Irish Fairy Tales, Myths & Legends

Kieran Fanning

For my parents,

Mary and Jim Fanning.

Thank you.

Irish Fairy Tales, Myths & Legends

Kieran Fanning

SCHOLASTIC

Published in the UK by Scholastic, 2020
1 London Bridge, London, SE1 9BG
Scholastic Ireland, 89E Lagan Road, Dublin Industrial Estate,
Glasnevin, Dublin, D11 HP5F

ISBN 978-93-5471-922-6

A CIP catalogue record for this book is available from the British Library.

www.scholastic.co.uk
First edition June 2020
This reprint edition June 2024
Printed in India at Shivam Offset Press, New Delhi

Contents

Fairy Tales and Folklore

The Mythological Cycle

The Ulster Cycle

The Fenian Cycle

Fairy Tales and Folklore

The fairy tales and folklore of this section were part of an oral tradition of storytelling long before they were written down. A seanchaí (storyteller) would have travelled from village to village telling these stories around firesides. With no television, internet or even electricity, this was a highly prized form of entertainment. The stories often contained supernatural creatures like the banshee, fairies, leprechauns and the devil. Repetition, magic and talking animals were also common features.

The King's Secret

This is a story about Labhraidh Loingseach (pronounced Lowry Lynshock). As a child, he stopped speaking, after witnessing the murder of his father and grandfather. For a long time he remained dumb, until he got hit on the shin during a game of hurling and cried out, "I'm hurt!" From then on he was called "Labhraidh", which means "he speaks" in Irish.

There once was a king of Ireland called Labhraidh Loingseach. He had unusually long hair that flowed around his shoulders in dark curls. He also wore an unusually high crown that made him appear taller than he was. The long hair and high crown were not fashion statements, but were there to hide a terrible secret, which if discovered, could end his reign as king.

You see, the king had been born with horse's ears instead of ordinary human ones. They hung on each side of his head but pricked to attention when he was straining to listen. The long hair was to hide the ears when they were hanging down, and the crown was to hide them when they were standing up.

When Labhraidh went to war, he wore a bronze helmet with two horns on top to hide his ears. When he went swimming, he wore a cloth cap in which he stuffed his hair and ears. People thought his head-gear was unusual but nobody said anything – kings were allowed to be a bit eccentric.

Once a year, the king had his hair cut in a private

room by a barber, often invited from far away. The barbers were always honoured to be invited to the royal court to cut the king's hair, but if they could have known what was going to happen to them, they most certainly would have refused.

Because, while cutting the king's hair, the barber would discover the king's secret and, while shocked by the discovery, the barber was even more shocked that the king never swore him to secrecy.

The reason the king wasn't worried about his secret getting out was because he made sure each barber was killed after cutting his hair. Many barbers went in through the king's front door, but none ever came out.

After many years, word got out that anybody who cut the king's hair never lived to tell the tale. Barbers abandoned their jobs or worked in secret, for fear of being summoned to Labhraidh Loingseach's royal fort to cut his hair.

It became so difficult to find a barber in Ireland that people had to let their hair grow so long that they tripped over it.

Every year, the king found it more and more of a challenge to find a barber. When his royal servants did find one, the barber never wanted the job and would plead to be excused. The servants, however, were under orders not to return to Labhraidh Loingseach's fort empty-handed, so they drew their weapons and escorted reluctant barbers to their last-ever job.

One such barber who was summoned went by the name of Marcán. When his mother, a widow, heard that her only son had been brought to cut Labraidhh Loingseach's hair, she was distraught and followed the cavalcade to the royal fort. She pleaded with the guards to let her in, where she found Marcán, scissors in hand, about to cut the king's hair.

"Your Majesty," she said, bowing down before the king. "Please ensure that no harm comes to my boy. He is all I have left in the world, and if he were to die, I think I would too."

"I don't know what you're talking about, woman," replied the king. "Your son has only been brought here to cut my hair."

"No offense intended, Your Majesty, but the whole world and its mother know that any barber that enters this place never leaves."

The king bowed his head in shame, for he didn't know that this was public knowledge. His servants had kept that from him as well as the fact that barbers were in short supply.

"Can your son keep a secret?" asked Labhraidh.

"Of course," said the widow, looking at Marcán, who nodded nervously.

"I give you my word," said the king, "that no harm will come to your son, if he promises to keep secret all he sees here."

"I promise," said Marcán.

"Good enough," said Labhraidh, removing his crown. "Now, leave us, woman. I want to get my hair cut in peace."

Tears of joy made the widow's eyes glassy as she bowed with gratitude and left her son to do his job.

Marcán removed his scissors and sharpened the blades on a whetstone. Then, he began cutting the king's hair.

As the dark curls fell to the floor, the boy spied something in the hair on each side of the king's head.

"Your Majesty. . ." mumbled the barber.

"Speak up, boy," said the king, whose ears, straining to hear, stood erect on his head.

Marcán gasped and stumbled backwards, dropping his scissors to the floor.

"Now you know the king's secret," said Labhraidh.

"And for that, you should be put to death. But I vowed to your mother that no harm would come to you, and I'll keep my promise if you keep yours."

"I promise I won't tell a living person what I've seen here," said Marcán.

The barber finished cutting the king's hair, and Labhraidh, happy with the job, said, "I appoint you Royal Barber, to return once a year to cut my hair."

Marcán nodded.

"Just remember your promise, boy."

Marcán bowed and left, not only with a handsome reward for his services, but with his life, relieved and grateful.

The people of Marcán's village were gobsmacked to see him return home, for they were sure he was a dead man.

"He must be a mighty fine barber," they said.

The next morning there was a queue of people outside Marcán's house waiting to have their hair cut, though many of them didn't need it. Some of them were even bald!

As Marcán snipped and trimmed, the customers plagued him with questions about the eccentric king, but Marcán's lips were sealed.

Over time, his fame grew far and wide. There was a constant queue outside his door. Everybody wanted to have their hair cut by the Royal Barber.

Marcán became a wealthy man, but he was not happy. The king's secret weighed heavily upon him, keeping him awake at night and putting him off his food. He would have no peace until he shared the secret. You know what they say: a burden shared is a burden halved.

He went to a local druid for advice.

"A secret will burn a hole in your heart," said the holy man. "The only cure is to share it."

"But I promised the king."

"What exactly did you promise him?"

Marcán squinted his eyes, trying to remember the exact words. "I promised not to tell a living person what I saw."

"A living person," repeated the druid. "That doesn't mean you can't tell a rock, a tree, a river or animal. Go into the forest and find something to share your secret with. The very act of saying the words out loud will ease your burden."

Marcán did as the druid instructed, and went deep into the forest until he was sure he was alone. Then, leaning into a walnut tree, he whispered his secret into its bark. "The king has horse's ears."

Immediately, he felt better, as if a crushing boulder had been lifted from his back.

He whispered it again. "The king has horse's ears. The king has horse's ears."

Each time he said it, he felt a little better. He kept saying it until he felt like a new man, released from prison. He skipped and sang the whole way home.

Not long after this, one of Ireland's most renowned harpists, Craiftine, happened to be in the very same forest sourcing wood to make a new harp. As soon as he saw the handsome walnut tree, he knew it would be perfect for his new instrument. He cut it down and carved the wood into a beautiful harp. When it was polished, the grain gleamed like golden veins.

He had just finished decorating the harp's pillar with carved Celtic knotwork and inset gemstones, when he received an invitation to play for none other than the king himself, Labhraidh Loingseach. Craiftine felt honoured to be invited.

A perfect opportunity to showcase my new harp, he thought, packing it carefully into a leather bag.

The harpist arrived at Labhraidh Loingseach's fort, marvelling at the splendour of the feast. Long tables were laden with succulent roast meat, fruit and vegetables. Mead and the finest imported wine flowed from intricately carved goblets, and the sound of laughter and conversation filled the air. The king's great hunting dogs prowled between the tables looking for scraps, while jugglers and acrobats entertained the guests.

After the feasting was over, the king clapped his hands, calling for music. Craiftine took his place on a low stool at the top of the hall and removed his magnificent new harp from its bag. He took a deep breath and placed his fingers on the strings.

When he plucked them, however, he didn't hear the usual melodic harp notes, but a high-pitched voice.

"The king has horse's ears. The king has horse's ears," sang the harp.

The guests gasped and then fell silent.

Craiftine removed his fingers from the strings but the harp continued to sing, "The king has horse's ears. The king has horse's ears."

Labhraidh Loingseach was so stunned that he shot to his feet, sending his crown flying and revealing his two tall horse's ears standing up on his head listening to the harp.

He expected everybody to laugh, point and mock,

but nobody did, for now they all knew the reason for Labhraidh's unconventional headgear and long hair. Many felt sorry that their king had such a burden to bear. This was the moment Labhraidh had dreaded all his life, but now that his secret was known, he felt free. Just as the barber had experienced, it was a relief to have it out in the open.

From that day on, the king wore his horse's ears with pride. He was happy, which meant his subjects were happy, especially the barbers who crawled out of hiding to give the people of Ireland much needed haircuts.

King Corc and His Daughter

Ireland has a rich heritage of folklore, including stories that only existed in oral form and were passed down from one generation to the next. Worried that these tales might be lost if they weren't written down, the Irish government asked school children to collect stories in their own localities. From 1937–1939, 740,000 pages of folklore were recorded in writing by pupils from 5,000 primary schools. This is one of those stories.

Just outside Cork City, there is a huge lake, and underneath the sparkling surface, the battlements and turrets of a great castle can be seen. It is said that a King Corc once owned the palace, and it was one of the finest royal establishments in the area. It had servants aplenty to tend to the king's guests' every need. Enormous, lush gardens surrounded the palace, and majestic peacocks strutted across its courtyards.

King Corc's most-prized possession, however, was a well in the centre of the palace. It produced the clearest, freshest drinking water in the land, and its fame had spread so far that, every day, people travelled great distances to taste its water. It was said that the water could cure all manner of sickness and injury.

Corc, however, was growing tired of the queues of poor and sick people ruining the beauty of the royal gardens. It annoyed him that they were taking his water for free.

"Soon, the well will probably run dry!" he spat.

One day, in a fit of rage, he ordered the people

waiting for the well to leave and never come back. Then, he commanded that a high wall be built from the castle, around the well, so that it could only be accessed from inside the palace. As added protection he locked the well behind a heavy gate.

The wall was built, and upon it, notices were posted that use of the well was forbidden and anyone who disobeyed would be severely punished. Corc locked the gate and gave the only key to his daughter, named Fíoruisce, which means "true water". He had named her after the well's water, so it was only fitting that she should be the guardian of the key.

The poor and sick people in Corc's kingdom were horrified at the king's actions and cursed their mean and hard ruler.

"He shall have no luck for his selfishness," they said.

But as time went on, King Corc continued to live happily in his rich palace.

One evening, a few years after the king had walled off the well, Corc arranged a great ball for all his rich and powerful friends. Kings, queens, princes and princesses travelled from the four corners of Ireland to attend this important event. Only those with a written invitation were allowed in.

As the guests filtered inside, a man in fine clothes rode a magnificent white horse up to the gates. He said he had come for the ball, but had no invitation. The guards didn't turn him away because he looked and sounded like royalty. Instead, they sent word to the king that a well-dressed stranger was requesting admission.

Corc and Fíoruisce came to a window to inspect the visitor.

"He is so handsome," said Fíoruisce, fixing her hair.

"And look at his finely tailored clothes," said the king.

"He must be a prince," said Fíoruisce, excitedly. "Oh, Father, please let him in."

The king nodded and sent word out to the guards to open the gates.

"Go and put on your best dress and jewellery," said Corc to Fíoruisce, who hurried away quickly.

Corc smiled as he watched his daughter run off to get changed. He couldn't understand why a prince had never proposed to her. She always wore the most expensive clothes and was rich beyond compare. What the king didn't realize was that when young men looked at her they didn't see the gold tiara and silk dress, but the mean-spirited and haughty personality she'd inherited from her father.

Perhaps this will be her lucky night, thought Corc, heading off to mingle with the guests.

The party was in full swing by the time he got to his banqueting hall. Jugglers tossed flaming torches into the air, while acrobats cartwheeled across the floor. The atmosphere was laced with excited chatter and giddy laughter. Steaming platters of roasted meat and vegetables were served to the guests on long candlelit tables.

Fíoruisce, who sat with her father on a dais at the top of the hall, hadn't touched her food. She was too busy looking at the dark-haired stranger who ate quietly at the bottom of the hall.

"I think I'm in love," she whispered to her father.

He laughed. "That's not the first time I've heard that."

"This time, I mean it. I bet he lives in a huge castle and has more gold than he can count."

When the meal was over, the music started and the dancers took to the floor. Fíoruisce couldn't believe it when the dark stranger rose from his seat, and crossed the dance floor, heading straight for her. Up close, he was even more handsome, and his clothes, even more impressive.

"Would the lady like to dance?" he asked, extending an open hand towards her. His voice was deep and crystal clear, like the very water that Fíoruisce had been named after.

With her cheeks now turning a rich crimson, she nodded and stood, hoping her legs wouldn't buckle with nerves. As the gentleman led her out into the centre of the floor, Fíoruisce knew all the ladies were watching her enviously. Already, she was planning what her wedding dress would look like. Indeed, she was so smitten with her dancing partner that she didn't notice the peculiar, wild light in his green eyes.

They danced and danced until they were out of breath, and joined the king at his table.

"Have a drink," said Corc, pouring the young man a cup of wine.

"Thank you," he said, "but my thirst is too great for wine. I don't suppose you have any water?"

The king leaned back in his gilded throne and laughed. "Not only do I have water, but I have the finest water in the whole of Ireland. It's as fresh as morning dew and as sweet as summer rain. A single mouthful can cure ill health and disease, as well as prolong the life of the drinker."

"This is something I must taste," said the stranger, searching the table.

"Oh, you won't find it here, for we keep it locked away. The princess has the only key."

He gestured to his daughter, who pulled out a gold chain from around her neck as if they'd rehearsed it. A heavy key dangled on the end of the chain.

Hoping that a romantic walk to the well might be just what his daughter needed to secure a marriage proposal, the king said, "Fíoruisce, take this young man to our well to taste the best water that's ever wet his lips."

The princess, more than happy to oblige, took the stranger's hand.

"Take a cup," said the king.

"No need," said the man. "I have my own."

He reached into his jacket pocket and produced a goblet of pure gold, inset with glittering jewels. Father and daughter were so mesmerized by the beautiful goblet that they didn't stop to think why somebody would be carrying such a thing in his jacket.

Fíoruisce led her dancing partner across the hall,

soaking up the green-eyed stares of the other single ladies. In the dark courtyard, the night air chilled her bare arms. She shivered and said she wanted to return for a shawl, but her companion hurried her forwards. Gripping her hand tighter, he pulled the princess towards the well.

Her hand shook as she put the key into the lock and opened the gate. Inside, the light from a single candle illuminated the well, and also the face of the stranger, which no longer seemed handsome or princely.

"I want to go back to my father," said Fíoruisce.

"You promised you'd fetch me a cup of water," said the man, handing her the golden goblet.

Now, she saw the strange green light flickering in his eyes and she was afraid.

When she took the goblet she felt a powerful energy vibrate inside it. It was pulled towards the well by some invisible force, dragging the princess with it. She tried to drop the cup, but it was stuck to her fingers. When the goblet reached the well, the water rushed upwards to meet it in an almighty torrent, whipping the cup away and knocking the princess off her feet.

Faster and faster the water spilled from the well,

rushing like an ocean wave into the corridors, carrying Fíoruisce with it.

The flood smashed open the doors of the banqueting hall and washed the princess up at the king's feet. He pulled his soaking daughter to her feet and asked her what had happened.

"The well," she spluttered. "It's overflowing."

By now the water had completely flooded the hall, and guests, musicians and servants screamed as the water rose higher and higher.

"We'll all be drowned," gasped the king.

Then he spotted the dark stranger with the green eyes sitting on Corc's throne, which was now floating like a little boat. The man was smiling.

"Make it stop!" ordered the king.

"Only you have the power to do that," said the stranger.

King Corc glanced around frantically at his guests, who were now waist-deep in water. "I'll do whatever it takes."

"This water belongs to the land and its people," shouted the stranger. "You had no right to lock it away behind a wall. Throw open your gates and give the water back to those who need it."

The king ordered every gate and door to be

opened, and soon the well's water flowed out over the flagstones of the courtyard and into the gardens and fields beyond. It gave the king and the princess time to escape from the castle, bringing with them their guests, staff and animals.

They climbed to the top of the nearest hill and watched the water flow across the valley. Indeed, it didn't stop flowing until it had completely covered the king's trees and castle, becoming a magnificent lake.

Having learned their lesson, the king and princess spent the rest of their lives telling everybody about the magical properties of their water. They encouraged sick, blind and crippled people from far and wide to bathe in their lake. Many of them emerged from the cool water completely cured, and forever grateful to King Corc and his daughter.

The dark stranger with the green eyes was never seen again.

The Twelve Wild Geese

"The Twelve Wild Geese" is an example of an international wonder tale. Various countries have versions of it that include children being turned into doves, ravens and ducks. "The Twelve Wild Geese" is particular to Ireland, and was published by the folklorist Patrick Kennedy in The Fireside Stories of Ireland *in 1870.*

There was once a queen who had twelve sons, and though she loved each one of them, she longed for a daughter more than anything in the world. One day, she gazed out her window to where a calf had been butchered on the newly fallen snow, in preparation for a banquet later that week. As the queen watched, she saw a raven land beside the carcass to peck at the spilled blood.

"I'd swap my twelve sons for a daughter with skin as white as snow, cheeks as red as blood, and hair as dark as a raven," said the queen.

The words had no sooner passed her lips than a wind howled into the room as if a window had been opened to a storm. The queen spun around to find an old woman with a long, crooked nose standing in the room. Her eyes glittered like broken glass.

She waved her walking stick at the queen. "That was a wicked wish you made, and as punishment it shall be granted. You will have a daughter, but at the cost of your twelve sons."

Before the queen had time to take back her wish,

a gale swirled from the woman's stick, whipping cups, plates, curtains and cushions into a whirlwind around her. The queen's screams were drowned out by the smashing crockery. When the wind subsided, the witch had gone.

Soon after, as the witch had predicted, the queen became pregnant.

On the day her baby was due to be born, the queen locked her twelve sons into one of the castle's highest towers, and posted guards around it.

As soon as her baby girl was born, a familiar wind rushed through the castle, chilling the sweat on the queen's brow, ruffling the newborn baby's hair, and continuing down the corridors until it reached the guarded tower. It whistled between the guards' legs and under the heavy oak door. Moments later, twelve geese were seen flying out through the open window. The king unlocked the tower but found only the boys' clothes and a few white feathers inside. The queen was distraught, knowing that she was to blame for what happened. The king, and indeed everybody in his kingdom, mourned the loss of the twelve princes by dressing in black for a whole year.

The princess grew up to be a beautiful girl with snow-white skin, rosy red cheeks and ebony dark hair. Everybody in the castle vowed to protect the princess by not telling her about her twelve brothers. Being an only child, however, she was lonely, and when she sought the company of her parents she found them distant, for though she didn't know it, they were grieving sorely for their lost sons.

And so, the princess found friendship amongst the gardeners, servants and kitchen staff. Indeed, they got so used to her that they often didn't notice her presence, and spoke freely around her. One day, she overheard a servant telling another servant about the events that had happened on the day the princess was born, and how the twelve princes had been turned into geese.

That's why my parents are so miserable, she thought. *And it's all my fault.*

The princess resolved to find her brothers, whatever it took, and, stealing food from the kitchen, she sneaked out of the castle grounds.

She walked all day, deeper and deeper into the forest, until night descended and she feared she'd have to sleep outside. But then, she spotted a light in the distance, and following it, she came to a little wooden house.

Inside, she found a table set with twelve plates,

twelve knives and twelve forks, and upstairs, twelve beds in a row.

She jumped at the sound of the door opening downstairs, and hurrying down, she found twelve men who looked so alike they had to be brothers.

"Who are you?" one of them asked.

When she told them, they all looked at each other and burst into tears. Here was their long-lost sister, who in their hearts, they loved, even though she was the reason for their banishment.

"You're my brothers, aren't you?" said the princess.

They nodded.

"But I thought you'd been turned into geese?" she asked.

A man, who appeared to be the oldest of the brothers, stepped forward. "We take the form of birds during daylight hours."

The princess felt tears welling behind her eyes. "My parents' hearts have been broken since you left. Please return, so that at least during the hours of darkness, they may see their sons."

"We would if we could, but the curse that turned us into birds also prevents us from ever seeing our parents."

As they wondered what to do, a wind pushed

open the door, blowing leaves and branches inside. When it died down, an old woman with a crooked nose stood in the doorway.

"The princess has proved her love for you, her brothers," she croaked, "so I have decided to lift your banishment and curse, under one condition."

"What is it?" asked one of the men.

"Your sister must spin and weave twelve shirts for you out of bog cotton, to be collected by her, and her alone. If she once speaks, laughs or cries during this time, the twelve of you will remain geese for the rest of your days."

With that, the wind whipped up the leaves into a cloud, and the witch disappeared.

Determined to break the curse, the princess stayed with her brothers, never laughing, crying or speaking a single word. She spent her days collecting the tiny tufts of bog cotton that grew sparingly in the surrounding forest and moors. She spent her nights spinning and weaving it into cloth. After three long years, she had completed eight shirts.

One day, while her brothers were up in the clouds, she met a handsome prince in the forest. He thought she was the most beautiful girl he'd ever seen, and he asked her to marry him. She, too, fell in love, and though she couldn't speak, she replied with a nod of her head. Using sign language, she told him that she needed to return to her house first.

There, she retrieved two baskets, one containing the eight cotton shirts, and the other containing bog cotton. As they rode off through the forest, the princess dropped a trail of bog cotton so that her brothers would find her.

The prince's palace was every bit as grand as he had promised. Everybody was happy to see the prince so in love, except for his stepmother, who took an immediate dislike to the mute girl who dressed in rags and spent her nights weaving bog cotton.

Despite his stepmother's misgivings, the prince married the princess, and before a year was out, she gave birth to a beautiful baby boy. The prince's father, the king, was overjoyed to have a grandchild. As much as the wicked stepmother hated the princess, she hated the baby even more because the king was spending more time with the baby than her. The stepmother made up her mind to get rid of the child.

One day, a hungry-looking wolf appeared in the royal gardens, and the stepmother decided to make the most of the opportunity. She put a sleeping potion in a cup of tea and brought it to the princess who was feeding her baby.

The princess smiled and nodded her thanks.

Having drained the cup, she fell into a deep sleep. With an evil grin, the stepmother stole the baby from his mother's arms and brought him out into the garden. Looking around to check that she hadn't been seen, she placed the child on the ground and ran back inside the castle. She watched through a window as the wolf snatched the baby into its jaws and fled into the forest.

The stepmother raced back upstairs, pricked her own finger with a needle and dabbed her blood around the sleeping princess's mouth. Then, she ran off to find the prince.

"Your Majesty," she said in a panicked voice. "You must come quickly. I fear your wife has done something terrible to your baby."

"What do you mean?"

"I think she may have eaten it."

Though he saw the blood on her mouth, the prince couldn't believe his wife could have done such a thing. When she woke up, she shook her head in denial of the accusation, but had no explanation for the missing child or the blood on her lips. The prince put out word that his child had been stolen, which though he did not know it, was sort of true.

The princess was the most unhappy woman in the kingdom, for she grieved not only for the loss of her parents and brothers, but now her own child. And to make matters worse, she could neither shed a tear nor speak about it. All she could do was continue to gather bog cotton and spin and sew as fast as she could. She looked often for her brothers but never saw the twelve wild geese that soared above the treetops keeping an eye on their little sister.

As time passed, the princess's grief for her lost son didn't diminish. But the task to free her brothers distracted her, and before long she had two pieces of good news to celebrate. One, she was almost finished weaving the twelve shirts. Two, she was pregnant again.

In time, the princess gave birth to a beautiful baby girl.

The wicked stepmother now hated the princess more than ever.

The prince may not have believed his wife had eaten their first baby, thought the stepmother wickedly. *But if the exact same thing happens a second time, he'll have to believe it.*

By some strange stroke of luck, the same hungry

wolf appeared in the garden just like the previous time. The stepmother drugged the princess, stole the baby and gave it to the wolf, which carried it away into the forest. Then, she pricked her finger and dabbed blood around the sleeping princess's mouth, just like the first time.

This time, when the prince saw the evidence, he was so frightened and upset that he ran away into the woods, leaving his wife in the hands of the wicked stepmother. Delighted there was no one to stop her, the stepmother took charge immediately and had the princess tried before a court of judges for the murder of her two children.

Unable to speak to defend herself, the princess was found guilty as charged. When she didn't cry or scream or protest her innocence, it made her look even guiltier. But in her heart, she screamed in anger at her evil stepmother, at the injustice of the world. In her heart, she also wept for her lost children. It was enough to make anyone fall down and die of sadness. Only one thing kept her going throughout all the misery, and that was the thought of her twelve brothers flying in the clouds, waiting to be rescued. Throughout the trial she clutched tightly to the eleven shirts she'd spent the past five years making.

The princess was sentenced to be burned alive. Determined to finish the final shirt and free her brothers before she died, the princess sewed night and day without a break, continuing to sew even as she was brought to the pyre on which she was to be burned. As her feet and neck were tied to a stake on top of a pile of dry wood, the princess finished stitching the final arm on the final shirt.

Just as she completed the last stitch, the executioner lit his torch, holding it close to the wooden pile.

Now she had completed the task, at last the princess was free to speak, and she shouted out in a cracked voice, "I'm innocent! Find my husband and I will prove it!"

The crowd gasped at the sound of the princess speaking for the first time. Everybody froze, except for the prince's stepmother, who grabbed the torch from the executioner and set the pyre alight before anyone could stop her.

The princess screamed as smoke billowed into the sky, where dark shapes were descending rapidly. Twelve wild geese landed on the pyre, flapping their wings to put out the flames.

"Put these on!" shouted the princess, throwing the cotton shirts into the air.

The geese wiggled their necks into them and, one by one, transformed into twelve young men, ready to rescue their sister. The crowd watched in amazement as the men untied the princess from the stake, and when the wicked stepmother tried to escape, one of them struck her on the head with a piece of wood. She fell to the ground and didn't get back up. The crowd cheered.

At that moment, a gust of wind churned into a blizzard of leaves at the edge of the clearing, and from the centre of it emerged an old woman with a crooked nose and a walking stick. On her back, she wore the pelt of a wolf, and in one of her arms she carried a newborn baby. The prince followed her, holding a little boy by the hand.

"My children," shouted the princess, running towards them.

She kissed her daughter and son and said to the old woman, "I thought they'd been eaten by a wolf."

The old woman smiled. "Wolves are not all bad."

"You rescued my children. I thought you were a witch."

"Witches are not all bad, either."

Next, the princess kissed her husband. "I can explain."

The prince glanced at the lifeless body of his step-mother. "No need, my love. This old woman who rescued your children has told me everything."

When they turned around to thank her she was gone. Where she had been standing, a wolf skin lay on the ground.

One by one, the princess's twelve brothers stepped forward to greet their new niece and nephew.

The next day, the princess, her husband, her two children and her twelve brothers set out on fourteen horses to visit an old king and queen who also had lost children.

If any family ever deserved happiness it was this one, and they made the most of it, by never making foolish wishes again. Sometimes, what you already have is just enough.

The Lazy Beauty and Her Aunts

This is an Irish version of the famous Rumpelstiltskin story. Indeed, the tale appears in the folklore of many different countries. It is called "Tom-Tit-Tot" in England, "Whuppity Stoorie" in Scotland and "Gillitrutt" in Iceland. "The Lazy Beauty and her Aunts" was published in The Fireside Stories of Ireland *by Patrick Kennedy in 1870.*

There was once a widow who was one of the hardest-working women in her town. She was particularly skilled on the spinning-wheel. She would spin and weave and sew clothes all day, every day, to earn a few shillings to feed her family.

Her only daughter, Anna, was not much help to her. She was as pretty as a summer's day, but as lazy as sin, and as useful about the house as a bucket with a hole in it. The widow tried enticing her with rewards, and when that failed, punishing her for her lazy attitude, but nothing worked. Anna stayed in bed half the day, and when she did get up, was so slow doing her few chores that it was quicker for her mother to do them herself.

One morning, the widow was outside rinsing some clothes in a barrel of water. It was midday and Anna was still in bed.

"You're a terrible girl!" the widow shouted into the cottage. "Get out here at once."

Now, who happened to be riding by and hear the widow shouting, but the queen's son? He rode up to the cottage to find out what the commotion was.

As he reached it, Anna emerged through the door, rubbing the sleep from her eyes. The prince thought she was the most beautiful girl he'd ever seen.

"Surely you weren't scolding this elegant maiden?" said the prince to the widow, while nodding at Anna.

The widow, trying to save herself and her daughter from embarrassment, curtsied for the prince and said, "Not at all, Your Majesty. In fact, I was scolding her for working too hard."

"Really?" asked the prince, becoming more interested. "Hard working, as well as beautiful. That is a rare combination. What work do you do, Anna?"

Now she had told one lie, the widow found herself carrying on down the path of lies. "She spins three pounds of flax a day, weaves it into linen the next day, and makes it into clothes the following day."

The prince couldn't believe it. His own mother, the queen, was one of the greatest spinners in the kingdom. She had rejected many a pretty girl that he had brought back to be his bride, merely because the girls couldn't spin. Yet, here was one who could spin expertly, and was also beautiful.

He turned to Anna. "You are one of the prettiest flowers I have ever seen. Would you do me the honour of escorting me home to meet my mother, and if she is agreeable, would you be my wife?"

Before the girl had a chance to answer, the widow said, "Yes, yes, yes. Of course she will."

She wasn't going to waste the chance of becoming a prince's mother-in-law. Grabbing her daughter's bonnet and cloak, she helped Anna on to the prince's horse.

The widow waved at the couple as they trotted off. Her heart was bursting with joy because she had honestly thought her daughter was too lazy to ever get married, and yet here she was riding off into the sunset with a prince, no less.

Though she thought Anna was pretty, the queen wasn't too pleased that the prince had chosen to bring home a poor country girl.

The prince, seeing the disappointment in his mother's eyes, said, "Anna is a wonderful worker. She can spin three pounds of flax in a day, weave it into linen the next day, and make it into clothes the following day."

"Really?" asked the queen, clearly impressed.

Anna nodded, because to tell the truth now would make a liar out of herself, her mother and the prince, and she'd grown rather fond of him in the short time they'd spent together.

The queen, however, wasn't the sort of woman to take someone's word for something. She needed to see it with her own two eyes. She needed proof.

"Please stay the night," she said to Anna, showing her to a grand bedroom. "And while you're here, you can spin these three pounds of flax into thread."

She pointed into the corner of the room at a spinning wheel and a pile of flax. Then, she shut and locked the door behind her.

Heavy-hearted, Anna sat down to spin, but the thread kept breaking. Why hadn't she paid more attention when her mother had showed her how to spin? Why hadn't she practised more at home?

In frustration, she threw down the flax and wept loudly, the tears making silvery trails down her cheeks.

"What's wrong, my girl?" asked a cracked voice from the middle of the room.

Anna was startled into silence, for standing in front of her was an old witch, dressed in black. She had rather small feet and a shrunken head, but wide hips and a huge backside. She was sort of shaped like a turnip, narrow at the top and bottom, but wide in the middle.

Anna explained how she had to spin the flax into thread before the morning.

"My name is Cailleach Cromáin Mór, and if you promise to invite me to your wedding, I will spin the flax into thread."

Anna agreed at once, and soon fell asleep in a huge four-poster bed to the sound of the old woman spinning. When she woke in the morning, the woman was gone and the flax had been spun into the finest gossamer thread.

The queen was so impressed that she invited Anna to stay another night. That evening, Anna couldn't eat much of the banquet that was laid on for her because she was anxious about what might be waiting for her in the bedroom later that night.

Sure enough, when the queen showed Anna to her room, she saw a mahogany loom in the corner beside the three-pound balls of thread.

"Let's see if you can turn this thread into linen by the morning," said the queen, before leaving and locking the door behind her.

Anna stood at the loom, but she didn't even know how to put the warp in the gears or how to use the shuttle. Afraid that she would lose the prince, who she was sure she loved, she started to cry.

"I will help you," croaked a voice in the room.

Anna looked up to see another witch. Like the

last one, she was old and dressed in black, but had huge hairy feet with no shoes on them.

"My name is Cailleach na Coise Móire, and I will turn this thread into linen if you promise to invite me to your wedding."

Anna nodded, and fell asleep to the sound of the loom's click-clack. When she awoke, the old woman was gone, and the thread had been woven into the finest linen.

The queen was so impressed that she invited Anna to stay for one final night.

That evening, as the queen escorted her to her room, Anna knew what would be waiting for her. Her fears were realized when she saw the pile of linen sitting in the corner with a scissors, needle and thread on top.

"If you turn this linen into clothes by the morning," said the queen, "you may marry my son before the month is out."

When she had left, Anna sat down and cried, for she knew she couldn't even thread a needle, never mind sew linen into clothes.

"Dry your tears, my girl," said a voice in the room.

Anna looked up to see an old witch with a big red nose.

"My name is Cailleach Srón Mhór Rua, and I will turn this linen into clothes if you promise to invite me to your wedding."

Anna said she would, and went to bed, leaving the old crone sewing in the corner. In the morning, Anna woke to find the witch was gone, and in her place, the most beautifully crafted linen shirts, trousers, jackets and dresses.

The queen was overjoyed.

She hugged Anna tightly. "We have a wedding to organize, my dear."

The prince, the queen and their servants did most of the organizing. All Anna really had to do was make a list of people she wanted to invite, but even that wasn't simple. She had promised the three witches an invitation, but now she wasn't so sure. She didn't know them, and what sane person would invite witches to a wedding?

She wondered why they wanted to come. Would they reveal her secret and ruin the wedding? It would be foolish to invite them, but breaking her promise might be even more dangerous. In the end, she decided to keep her word and put them on the guest list. A promise was a promise, after all.

As you can imagine, the wedding was a lavish

affair, with the finest food, wine, flowers, ribbons, music and dancing. Anna's mother, wearing a stunning satin and lace dress that she had made herself, beamed with pride. She realized she had lots in common with the queen: spinning, weaving, sewing, and now of course, Anna.

"She is an amazing seamstress," said the queen. "You taught her well."

Anna's mother tried not to choke on her wine.

At the other end of the table, the newly married couple sat, chatting to the guests who had formed a line to their table. Anna's face drained of colour when she saw the three witches join the queue. She was sure the women were going to reveal her secret. By the time the first of the witches reached the table, Anna was a nervous wreck.

The old turnip-shaped woman with wide hips and a huge backside bowed to the prince. Her head and feet looked too small for the rest of her body.

"Your Majesty," she said, "my name is Cailleach Cromáin Mór, and I am Anna's aunt."

"Pleased to meet you," said the prince. "Your name is unusual. What does it mean?"

"It means Old Woman of the Big Hips, on account of my large bottom."

The prince tried not to laugh. "Erm... How did your hips get so big?"

"From a lifetime of sitting at a spinning wheel."

The prince looked at his beautiful bride and said, "From now on, you are forbidden to sit at a spinning wheel."

Anna was too shocked to speak, so she just smiled and nodded.

Next in the queue was the second witch.

"My name is Cailleach na Coise Móire, and I am Anna's aunt."

"Pleased to meet you," said the prince. "Your name is also unusual. What does it mean?"

"It means Old Woman of the Big Feet."

The prince glanced down at the woman's enormous feet. "Why are they so big?"

"From a lifetime of standing at a loom."

"In that case," said the prince to his bride, "you are forbidden from ever standing at a loom."

Again, Anna just smiled and nodded.

Next in line was the third witch. She had a big red nose.

"My name is Cailleach Srón Mhór Rua, and I am Anna's aunt."

"Pleased to meet you," said the prince. "What

does your name mean?"

"Old Woman of the Big Red Nose."

The prince nodded, as if to say he should have guessed. "How did your nose become so big and red?"

"A lifetime of leaning over my stitching sent the blood into my nose, making it big and red."

The prince looked at his wife's pretty little nose and said, "From now on, you are forbidden from stitching. I never want to see a needle or thread in your hand."

Anna nodded and sighed with relief. Her secret was still safe, and thanks to the witches she'd never have to spin, weave or sew again. She truly was the luckiest girl in the world.

The princess lived happily ever after with the prince, and whenever she had a party she always invited her three new aunts.

The Lady of Gallarus

This is a story about a merrow, the Irish version of a mermaid. They were said to wear a magic cap that enabled them to travel between deep water and dry land. The cap was called a "cochaillín draíochta" which translates from Irish as "little magic hood". The merrow is not to be confused with the selkie, another mythological creature that appears in Irish and Scottish stories. Selkies could change from seal to human form by shedding their skin.

In Gallarus, in the county of Kerry, there once lived a man named Richard Fitzgerald. He was a lonely man, and all he wanted was a wife and maybe a few children. Being unmarried, he felt like a dance without music, or a pair of scissors without one of its legs. In short, his life felt incomplete.

One day, he was sitting on the shore of his town's harbour, looking out at the sea and smoking his pipe. The water was as green and tranquil as polished marble, and the smoke from Richard's pipe curled around his head in little clouds.

As he gazed along the beach, he saw a most extraordinary sight. A creature had been washed up on the shore. At first, he thought it was a huge fish because its tail, covered in iridescent scales, flapped in the sand. But then he saw that the tail was attached to the body of a woman. With long golden hair, she was more beautiful than anyone he'd ever seen.

Upon her head, she wore a little red-feathered cap, and when she took it off and threw it in the sand nearby, a magical thing happened. The scales on her tail began to fade away and were gradually replaced with human skin. The fish-tail itself split in two, each piece contorting and convulsing until it took the shape of a human leg. In minutes, the woman had lost her tail and acquired a pair of legs. She sat on a rock, with her back to Richard, and began to comb her hair.

He knew what he was looking at was a merrow. Many a fisherman had been lured to his death while following one of these beautiful creatures underwater. Richard, however, would not be so easily tricked, for he knew that the merrow's power lay in its enchanted cap. It allowed her to transform from a human into a merrow, as well as breathe underwater. Without it, she couldn't escape.

Walking softly, he crept up behind her, and put the red cap in his pocket. When she heard him, she scuttled behind a rock in fear. He could see her eyes darting about the sand, looking for her cap, and not finding it, she began to sob great fat tears.

"Oh, please don't cry," said Richard, rushing up to her and holding her hand to soothe her.

She stopped crying instantly, blinking up at him.

"What is your name?" asked Richard.

"Muireann," she said. "Please don't eat me."

Richard laughed. "I'm not going to eat you."

"Then, what will you do with me?"

Richard looked down at her hand in his. The skin between her fingers was slightly webbed, but apart from that, it looked like a perfectly normal woman's hand. Everything about her looked normal, except that she was more beautiful than most. Nobody would know she was a merrow.

"I want you to be my wife," said Richard.

Muireann thought long and hard about the offer, before saying, "I'll be your wife if you give me back my cap."

Richard knew if he returned her cap she'd just pop it on her head and return to the water, never to be seen again. "I promise I'll give it back to you once we're married."

"It's a deal," she said, shaking Richard's hand.

Before they left, Muireann went to the water's edge and whispered something into the surf. Bubbles swirled in the water and got carried out to sea, as if they were the merrow's words.

"What are you doing?" asked Richard.

"Sending word to my father that I may not be home for some time."

"Who is your father?"

"He is king of the waves, and he'll be worried about me."

That means you're a princess, he thought, feeling even more pleased with himself to have found such an important wife.

He took her by the hand and led her straight off to the priest. The couple was married quietly and quickly.

When they got back to Richard's house, he waited until his wife was asleep before removing the little red cap from his pocket and putting it in a tin box. He crept outside in the dark and hid it in the potato pit, before returning to bed.

For the first few months, the married couple were content, and Muireann took to household duties happily, considering she'd spent her life living underwater. She cooked the dinner, cleaned the house and darned her husband's socks, and for a while, seemed satisfied with her lot, but soon became wistful and listless as homesickness took hold of her. Richard would often find her frozen in the middle of some task, as if turned to stone, her eyes always pointing out the window at the endless ocean.

One day, she said, "Husband, dear, I love you very much and if you love me the same way, you'll allow me to return home."

"Give it a year," said Richard, "and if there's nothing keeping you here, then, I'll let you go."

Muireann seemed happy with that. A while later, she became pregnant and gave birth to a baby girl called Kathelin. She loved her child like any mother would, but when the year was up, her desire to go home was stronger than ever.

"Husband, dear, please allow me to return to the sea."

"Our baby girl depends on you, my dear. Wait, at least, until she's a little older."

She said she would.

Every time Richard went out to the potato pit, he saw the tin box that contained the merrow's cap, and was often tempted to return it to her, but he knew if he did he'd lose her forever, so he kept it hidden.

Before another year had passed, Muireann gave birth to a boy, and afterwards, she asked her husband about going home.

His answer was the same. "Our new baby depends on you. Wait, at least, until he's a little older."

A few months later, Muireann became pregnant again, and gave birth to another boy. She loved her children very much, but the pull of the sea was even stronger. For the fourth time, she asked her husband to give her back her cap so she could return home. She wasn't surprised by his answer.

"You have three children who depend on you, my dear. Wait, at least, until they are a little older."

Muireann knew her husband would always have an excuse to refuse her, and in time, she gave up asking, though her homesickness grew more intense with every year that passed.

When she stopped asking to leave, Richard presumed she'd given up any hopes of returning home and, bit by bit, gave her more freedom. He allowed her into town alone to do shopping, or he sometimes went off on trips himself, not returning till nightfall or the next morning.

He was due to make another such trip and, before he went, Muireann asked him to fetch some potatoes from the pit. He said he would, but in his haste to pack a few belongings for the trip, he forgot. It was only when he'd gone that Muireann realized Richard hadn't brought in any potatoes.

She went out to the potato pit, and as she was throwing spuds into a basket, she spied a little tin box. As soon as she put her hand inside it, she knew what it was, because a tingling sensation ran up and down her legs. It was her little red cap!

Her thoughts immediately returned to her underwater home full of brightly coloured fish, and her father and mother sitting on their coral thrones, and her brothers and sisters sleeping in their oyster beds.

Her heart was pulled in that direction as if it had been hooked by a fishing line. It was also pulled in the other direction, back towards the cottage where her three children waited for their dinner. She couldn't abandon them, especially when their father was away and wouldn't be back till morning.

Stuffing the cap into her pocket, she brought the potatoes back to the house and made a fine dinner with bacon and cabbage. Afterwards, she took her children for a walk along the strand, and told them stories of merrows who lived under the sea.

"But merrows aren't real, are they?" asked Kathelin. "It's just a story."

"Was the story I just told you real?" asked her mother.

Kathelin nodded.

"Then, everything in it was real, too."

Kathelin smiled, not realizing the truth of her mother's words.

Later, Muireann tucked her three children into

bed and hid her red cap under her mattress. No matter how hard she tried, she couldn't sleep. The crashing of the surf outside her window seemed louder than normal. She felt the waves were singing her name, as if they were the tears of a heartbroken king and queen, crying for their lost daughter.

Unable to resist the temptation any longer, Muireann rose from her bed, and put the little red cap in the pocket of her nightdress. She went in to her two sleeping boys and kissed them on their foreheads. Then, she went to Kathelin's bed and did the same. When she leaned over, a tear fell from her eye and on to her daughter's cheek. The girl's eyes, heavy with sleep, opened a crack.

"I love you, my darling," whispered Muireann. "Look after your brothers."

Kathelin smiled, thinking she was still dreaming, before turning over and going back to sleep.

Outside, the moon shone brightly, lighting up the path to the beach. It made the foam-crested waves glow on the black sea, its lapping waves sounding like the whispers of Muireann's merrow family.

Once I've seen my parents, brothers and sisters, I'll return, she thought, looking back mournfully at the cottage where her children slept.

She slipped out of her nightdress, the breeze goose-bumping her skin. Then, taking her little red cap, she walked into the sea until the water rose over her ankles, then her knees, and then her thighs.

As soon as she placed the little red cap on her head, her legs started to tingle. She felt the skin on them move and harden, and beneath it, her bones and muscles shifted. She lost her balance and fell back into the water. Instead of her toes, feet and legs breaking the surface of the sea, she saw a fish tail, its scales shimmering in the moonlight.

For the first time in many a year, Muireann felt whole again – happy and at peace. She was a merrow. Flipping her tail, she disappeared under the water.

Richard Fitzgerald returned home in the morning to find Kathelin making breakfast for her brothers. There was no sign of Muireann. Kathelin told her father about the dream she'd had, in which her mother had told her to look after her brothers.

Fearing that it hadn't been a dream, Richard ran out to the potato pit, and finding the tin box empty, knew what had happened. For the rest of the day, he gazed out at the sea, waiting for her to return, and when she didn't, he did the same for the weeks and months that followed.

What he didn't know was that Muireann returned often, but stayed just beneath the surface of the water, where she watched her children play on the beach. How her heart ached to reveal herself, but she saw they were coping well without her, and knew if Richard got his hands on her cap a second time, she'd never escape.

As the years passed, she watched her children grow up and leave to make lives for themselves. Though she missed them sorely, she could see they were happy, and that pleased her.

With the children gone, Muireann didn't return as often, but once a year she swam to just beneath the surface to check on her husband. Though she didn't love him, she did feel sorry for him because he never married again, but spent his days watching the ocean, waiting for the return of his wife, the merrow that the locals now referred to as the Lady of Gallarus.

The Legend of Bottlehill

Many Irish place names have their origins in myth and legend. One such place is Bottlehill, which is between Mallow and Blarney, in County Cork, in the south of Ireland. The story of how Bottlehill got its name was originally published by the folklorist Thomas Croften Croker in his 1906 book, Fairy Legends and Traditions of the South of Ireland.

Near Mallow, a poor farmer called Mick Purcell lived with his wife and children. They rented a small farm from the local landlord and lived as simply as they could, only eating what they grew, but no matter how they scrimped and saved, paying the rent was always a problem.

One year, after a bad harvest, their chickens died of disease, and their pig got measles, and Mick didn't have enough money to pay the landlord his rent.

"What are we going to do, Molly?" he asked his wife.

"There's only one thing to do," she replied. "We'll have to sell the cow at the fair in Cork."

Reluctantly, Mick agreed, and he set out the next day with the cow. After a long, tiring walk, he came to the top of a steep hill and met a tiny man, no bigger than a small child. The man had white hair, reddish eyes, a sharp nose and slightly pointed ears.

Mick said hello politely but kept walking briskly because he feared the stranger was one of the Fairy Folk, and Mick knew better than to get involved with them.

The little man, however, followed Mick and soon they were walking side by side, though walking was probably the wrong word because the little man seemed to float along the road, his feet hidden under a long coat.

"Where are you going with the cow?" asked the stranger.

"I'm going to sell her at the fair in Cork."

"Will you sell her to me instead?"

Mick didn't want to have any dealings with the Little People, but to refuse could be dangerous. "How much will you give me for her?"

The old fairy pulled out a glass bottle from inside his jacket. "I'll give you this."

"An empty bottle? What good is an empty bottle? My wife will kill me if all I come home with is a glass bottle. A bottle won't feed my family or pay the rent."

"This bottle is worth more than any amount of money you'll get at the fair."

"I think I'll take my chances at the fair," said Mick.

"Take your chances all you want, but how do you know you'll get a good price at the fair? How do you know the cow won't die before you reach Cork?" The little man smiled a nasty grin, and Mick couldn't help but think the fairy was threatening him.

"Make up your mind, Mick Purcell," said the little fellow.

How does he know my name? thought Mick.

As if reading his mind, the fairy said, "I know all about you, Mick Purcell. Now what's it to be?"

Out of fear, Mick handed over the cow.

The little man gave him the glass bottle in exchange. "When you get home, put the bottle on the table and say the words 'Bottle, do your duty', and you will get what you deserve."

Mick thanked the man and began to retrace his steps towards home. When he glanced behind him and saw that the little man and the cow had completely disappeared, Mick knew for sure that he'd just done a deal with one of the Sídhe, the Fairy Kind of Ireland.

He hurried home and surprised his wife, who was sweeping the floor.

"Mick, you can't have been to Cork and back already?"

"I sold the cow to a man on the road."

"And how much did you get for her?"

"This." Mick pulled the bottle out of his jacket.

"An empty bottle? You sold our cow for an empty bottle! What sort of fool are you, Mick Purcell?" She clattered him across the back with the broom.

When she calmed down, Mick told her the whole story. "The bottle is magic, you see."

"Hmmm," said Molly, unconvinced. "Let's see."

Mick placed the bottle in the middle of the table and said, "Bottle, do your duty."

Mick and Molly's children gasped as a twinkling light swirled around inside the bottle, and then from the neck of it, emerged a little man's head. Molly stepped back from the table in terror, as the little man lifted himself out of the bottle, and then reached in to pull a companion out, identical in size and appearance.

Together, the two sprites began pulling tiny golden plates and dishes out of the bottle. They grew to full size once they were placed on the table. Then, the men pulled out silver knives, forks and spoons. After that, they produced the most marvellous assortment of foods from the bottle – roast beef, boiled ham, honeyed vegetables, creamy mashed potatoes, apple tart and plum pudding. When the table was covered in food, and the air sweet with delicious smells, the two tiny men disappeared back into the bottle.

"I told you the bottle was magic," said Mick, dancing around the room.

That night, the family dined like royalty, licking every crumb off the golden plates.

With the children now in bed, Molly said, "Indeed, your bottle is magic, Mick, but we can't exactly pay the landlord with roast beef or mashed potato."

Mick picked up one of the golden plates. "I bet this would fetch a pretty penny, though."

The next day, Mick took the plate to Cork, but made sure to go a different route so as to avoid the hill where he'd met the fairy. The plate turned out to be pure gold, and Mick sold it for more money than he ever had in his life. He was able to buy a new horse and cart and still have money left over to pay the landlord.

After that, the Purcells always had money to pay the rent. When they ran out of it they just sold another golden plate. When the plates ran out, they just commanded the bottle to do its magic. Indeed, they got so rich that they splashed out on cattle, jewellery and fancy clothes.

After a while, their landlord started to get suspicious. None of his other tenants were prospering so well on their tiny farms. He called around to ask Mick where he was getting the money from. Whether it was due to honesty or boastfulness, nobody knows, but Mick told his landlord all about his magic bottle. The greedy landlord offered Mick a great deal of money for the bottle, but Mick declined.

"Why would I sell the bottle for money," he said, "when it is, itself, a money-making machine?"

"Then sell it for something that money can't buy," said the landlord.

"What do you mean?"

"I'll give you your farm in exchange for the bottle. You'll never have to pay rent again."

Mick was so excited about the thought of never paying rent again that he accepted the offer without thinking carefully about it.

After that, things didn't go so well for the Purcells. Sure, they now owned their own farm, but the magic bottle had made them lazy, and soon they let the farm go to rack and ruin. It got to the stage that they didn't have enough food to feed the children.

"Mick," said Molly, "take our last cow to the hill where you met the little man and see if he has another magic bottle in exchange for the animal."

Mick did as he was told and returned to the hill in question, leading his cow on a rope.

Sure enough, the little man with the red eyes was there. "Well, Mick Purcell, how can I help you today?"

"I was wondering if you'd like to take my cow in exchange for another magic bottle?"

"Well, it just so happens that I have another bottle," said the fairy, pulling it out of his jacket and handing it to Mick. "You know what to do with it?"

Mick nodded and returned home with the bottle.

Placing it in front of his wife, he said, "Bottle, do your duty."

As before, a light twinkled in the bottle and a little man lifted himself out, before reaching in to pull out his companion. But instead of producing golden plates and food, they hopped down off the table and began racing round the kitchen, smashing Molly's crockery and pulling the curtains off the window. Mick chased after them but they giggled with glee as the slipped out of his grasp, knocking over a churn of milk and smashing the last of the eggs on the floor. One of them threw a sod of turf at the window, smashing the glass, while the other pulled a burning stick from the hearth and set fire to the cushions.

The children ran screaming out of the house. While Mick and Molly stamped out the flames on their cushions, the two little sprites squealed in delight as they broke the oil lamp, turned over the furniture and ripped the feathers out of the pillows. Indeed, they didn't return to the bottle until the whole house was trashed.

Molly glanced around at her kitchen, which looked like it had been visited by an angry bull. In despair, she lay on the ground and cried. Mick looked at the empty bottle on the table and remembered the old fairy's promise: "You will get what you deserve".

I got what I deserved, all right, he thought. *This is all my own fault. I had a perfectly good bottle and a way to make money forever, but I got greedy and threw it all away.*

Determined to make things right, he took the bottle to his old landlord, who happened to be throwing a party when Mick arrived.

"Mick Purcell, what can I do for you?"

"Oh, it's not what you can do for me, but what I can do for you," said Mick. "I brought you another bottle."

"Is it magic, like the last one?"

Mick nodded.

"Come in," said the landlord, leading him into a great hall full of wealthy guests.

Mick saw his old bottle up on a shelf.

"Show us what it can do," said the landlord.

Mick took the bottle out of his jacket, placed it on the floor and said, "Bottle, do your duty."

Out emerged the two little sprites, giggling in high-pitched laughter. The landlord and guests smiled in amazement, but only Mick Purcell knew what was going to happen next. Sure enough, the two little fairies began speeding around the room, smashing crystal glasses and fine-boned china off the walls. Everyone screamed as glass rained down on them, and they tried to catch the little creatures but they were too flighty for human hands.

The sprites turned over bookcases, pulled down the chandelier, poked holes in paintings, set the curtains alight, threw books on the fire, smashed window panes and cut holes in the upholstered furniture. In minutes, the room looked like it had been hit by a tornado.

"Make them stop!" shouted the landlord.

"Only if you give me back my old bottle," replied Mick.

"Take it!"

Mick waited until the two little fairies had finished destroying the place and returned to their bottle. Then he took both bottles home with him.

After that, Mick and Molly became very wealthy.

The Purcell children married into prosperous families and became rich too. Indeed, one of their sons married the landlord's only daughter. The landlord had spent such a fortune restoring his wrecked hall that he was too scared to mention the bottles ever again.

Mick and Molly lived to ripe old ages and both died on the same day. At their wake, a fight broke out among their servants and the two magic bottles were accidentally broken.

The little old fairy was never seen again, but from that day on, the hill became known as Bottlehill.

Jack and the Man in Black

This story features two characters that are prominent in Ireland's folklore. The devil often appears as a dark stranger with cloven hooves trying to win somebody's soul. The leprechaun is a type of fairy, probably descended from the Tuatha Dé Danann, a supernatural race of gods. They are usually depicted as mischievous, bearded shoemakers. If captured by a human they often give up their pot of gold or three wishes in exchange for their freedom.

Even as a child, Jack had always been different. He was always claiming he'd seen a fairy or a ghost. He even claimed he'd once seen a banshee, brushing her hair and crying a lament outside some unfortunate's house. Of course, nobody ever believed him.

By the time he reached adulthood, he hadn't changed much, and had little prospect of finding a wife or a job. His parents, worried that he'd amount to nothing, sent him to be an apprentice to a shoemaker in a nearby town. It was an honourable trade, and one you could make a fine living from.

For three years, Jack learned the craft, and when he was fully qualified, he headed for home. As darkness drew in, he decided to take a shortcut through a bog. While picking his step between treacherous bog holes, he heard a metallic clinking noise. He recognized it immediately as the sound of a shoemaker's hammer hitting a nail.

But who would be making shoes so late at night, and in a bog of all places? wondered Jack.

He followed the sound until he found a little man sitting on a rock. He had his back to Jack, who could see the little man wore a black three-cornered hat, a dark green coat and bright red stockings. He was mending a shoe which he held between his knees. Jack's mouth fell open in surprise. It was a leprechaun.

People said if you caught a leprechaun you could demand his crock of gold and live in riches for the rest of your days. Jack knew they were renowned for their tricks and would do anything to escape being caught or giving up their gold.

Holding his breath, he crept up behind the little man, thoughts of the pot of gold whirling in this mind. The leprechaun was so engrossed in his work that he didn't hear anything until it was too late.

Jack grabbed the little man by the shoulders and spun him around so they were facing each other. "I have you now, Mr Leprechaun."

"You have indeed," said the leprechaun, seeming not at all frightened.

He had an old face with a white beard, but the bright, lively eyes of a child.

"I suppose you're after my crock of gold?" asked the leprechaun.

"That, I am," said Jack.

"Well, I'm sorry to say that I don't have one. You

see, one of your Big People captured me last week and I had to surrender my treasure."

"I don't believe you."

"Well, if you know anything about the Little People, and I think you do, you'll know that we may not always tell the truth, but we never lie."

Jack frowned, trying to make sense of what the leprechaun had said. "I'm not letting you go until you give me something."

"I can give you my leather bag," said the leprechaun, nodding at a bag on the ground.

Jack picked it up with one hand, making sure to keep a tight grip of the leprechaun with the other. "Why would I want a leather bag that's too small to hold anything?"

"It's a magic bag that will grow big enough to hold anything you choose to put in it."

"Let's see if you're right," said Jack, pulling the bag down over the leprechaun's head.

It should only have been big enough to hold the little man's head, but as Jack pulled on it, the bag grew and grew until the leprechaun's whole body was inside.

"Do you believe me now?" shouted the leprechaun from inside the bag.

"I do," said Jack, letting the little cobbler out again. "A bag like this might be useful some day. I'll take it, in exchange for your freedom."

"May it bring you wealth and happiness," said the leprechaun, bowing low to the ground. "And with a bit of luck, may I never see you again."

Jack looked out into the darkness. "Be careful out there, little man. A bog is a dangerous place on a dark night. You really need someone with a lantern to guide you around the bog holes."

"Are you offering?"

Jack shook his head.

"Well then, I'm off," said the leprechaun, disappearing into the night.

Jack returned home and hung up his little leather bag and forgot all about it, concentrating instead on setting up his shoemaker shop.

At first, business thrived, and in fact, Jack turned out to be an excellent shoemaker. But that was part of the problem. You see, Jack's shoes were so well made that they lasted for a long time and his customers didn't need new shoes or repairs very often.

By the time winter came, business was slow, and Jack had to borrow money from his friends and family to buy food.

One day, a dark-haired stranger with very pink skin arrived in Jack's shop. He wore a black overcoat, a black hat and black trousers which were so wide you couldn't see his shoes. On his hands he wore black gloves with a gold ring on his little finger outside the glove.

"I'm looking for Jack," he said.

"I am Jack," said the cobbler. "How may I be of service to you?"

The man in black laughed. "It is I who can be of service to you. I heard you've been having some money issues?"

"Oh, nothing that I can't handle."

"What would you say if I told you I could give you all the money you could want, and enough business to make you the most famous shoemaker in Ireland?"

"I'd say, 'Where's the catch?' What would I have to do in return?"

"Something simple," said the stranger. "In seven years' time, you must come with me and ask no questions."

"Is that all?"

The man in black smiled and nodded.

"It's a deal," said Jack, sticking out his hand to shake the stranger's gloved hand.

The man in black then produced a bundle of cash and handed it over to Jack. "I'll see you in seven years' time."

When the stranger had gone, Jack noticed cloven hoof marks scorched into the floor where the man had been standing.

A terrible thought occurred to him. Was the man in black the devil? Had he just made a deal with Satan?

This worried him for a while, but then he became so busy in his shop that he put it out of his mind. Soon, he became known far and wide as being the best shoemaker in Ireland. He moved to a bigger house and was even able to employ apprentices and servants. Every now and then his thoughts wandered back to the deal he'd done with the man in black. Jack had promised to go somewhere with the devil in seven years' time. The shoemaker had a fair idea where that "somewhere" might be, and he didn't want to go.

By the time the seven years had passed, Jack had a plan in place. He just hoped it would work.

One day, one of his servants said, "Jack, there's a man dressed in black waiting in the shop to see you."

It was the day Jack had been dreading, but he was ready. He ran into the bedroom and fetched the leprechaun's little magic bag.

"I've been expecting you," said Jack, shaking hands with the man in black. "My bag is packed and I'm ready to go."

"You couldn't fit much in that bag. Let me have a look."

"All right," said Jack, opening the bag. "Just a quick look."

The man in black peered in. "It's empty."

"It is not. Look closely."

When the devil stuck his head inside, Jack pulled the bag over him. It expanded until the man in black was completely inside. Jack tied a knot on top.

"Let me out!" shouted the devil.

"I will if you declare our agreement over."

"Never!"

So Jack dragged the bag down the road to the blacksmith's forge.

"Jack," said the blacksmith, "they were a great pair of shoes you made me. How can I help you?"

"I've a bag of tin that needs softening," said Jack.

"Of course," replied the blacksmith, "but wouldn't it be better if we took the tin out of the bag?"

"No, it'll be perfectly fine in the bag."

The blacksmith nodded, dragged the bag on to his anvil and began beating it with his hammer.

When he'd finished, Jack pulled the bag down the road. "Will you declare our agreement over, now?"

"Never," mumbled the devil.

So, Jack continued down the road until he came to a mill.

"Jack," said the miller. "They were a great pair of shoes you made me. How can I help you?"

"I've a bag of corn that needs grinding."

"Of course," said the miller, "but wouldn't it be better if we took the corn out of the bag?"

"No, it'll be perfectly fine in the bag."

The miller nodded and placed the bag between the two huge mill stones. When they turned, they flattened the bag between them like a pancake.

Jack dragged the bag down the road. "Will you declare our agreement over, now?"

"Never," mumbled the devil.

So, Jack continued on until he came across a bunch of boys playing hurling.

"Jack," said the boys, "they were great hurling boots you made us. How can we help you?"

"I've a bag of hurling balls that need softening."

"Of course," said the boys, "but wouldn't it be better if we took them out of the bag?"

"No, they'll be perfectly fine in the bag."

The boys nodded and began beating the bag with their hurley sticks.

When they'd finished, Jack dragged the bag down the road. "Will you declare our agreement over, now?"

"OK!" shouted the devil. "I declare our agreement over."

Jack opened the bag, and the devil crawled out, black and blue with bruises.

"You're a terrible man, Jack. I never want to see you again." The devil twirled around on the spot and disappeared in a puff of smoke.

Jack went on to live a very long and prosperous life. He was over ninety when he died. Of course, he went straight to heaven, because he'd been such a good and honest shoemaker.

He rang a gold bell on heaven's pearly gates and waited for it to be answered.

An old man in white robes, and carrying a book appeared. "My name is Peter. Please state your own name and occupation."

"My name is Jack and I am a shoemaker."

Peter flipped through the pages of the book. "It says here that you made a deal with the devil?"

"I did," explained Jack, "but the devil ended our agreement. He said he never wanted to see me again."

Peter shook his head and closed the book. "A deal is a deal, Jack. Someone who promised his soul to the devil cannot enter heaven."

"So, where will I go?"

"There's only one other place you can go. Follow the road behind you." Peter turned and walked away into the clouds.

Jack followed the white brick road. As he walked, the bricks became redder and the light faded. By the time he reached the end of the road it was so dark he could barely see the red bricks under his feet.

A huge door stood before him, and through the keyhole and the cracks in the wood, Jack could see the flames of an intense inferno. He had arrived at hell.

The door was almost too hot to knock on.

When the devil opened the door, the fiery pink colour drained from his face.

"Ah, it's yourself," said Jack.

"I . . . I . . . I said I never wanted to see you again,"

the devil stuttered.

"It's not my fault. I died and was sent to heaven but Peter wouldn't let me in. He said I had to come here."

"You must be joking. I remember what you did to me the last time."

"So, where will I go?"

The devil pulled a big black book out and flicked through the pages. "It says here that you once said someone with a lantern should guide travellers through the bog at night."

"I remember!" said Jack. "I said it to the leprechaun!"

Satan snapped the book closed. "Well, then, that is what you shall do from this day forwards."

"But I don't have a lantern," said Jack.

The devil disappeared and returned moments later with a knife, a turnip and a burning ember from hell.

"Make one!" he shouted, throwing the items at Jack's feet and slamming the door to hell closed.

Jack hollowed out the turnip with the knife. He was so angry at the man in black that he carved the devil's face in the turnip and threw the burning ember inside to create a lantern.

It is said that Jack still roams the bogs of Ireland.

Many claim to have seen his lantern. Some people call him Stingy Jack. Others call him Jack o' the Lantern.

At Halloween, Irish people began carving lanterns with faces out of turnips. When Irish immigrants went to America they couldn't find turnips so they used pumpkins instead. This is where the tradition of carving a jack-o'-lantern comes from.

The Mythological Cycle

Myths are really old stories, often about gods or supernatural humans. Ireland's myths are thousands of years old and were passed from person to person by word of mouth, evolving as they went. They were eventually recorded in writing by Christian monks, some of whose manuscripts have survived to this day.

Nuada of the Silver Arm

According to the Book of Invasions, *a book of mythology written in the eleventh century, the Tuatha Dé Danann were one of the first people to come to Ireland. They were a supernatural race of gods and ruthless warriors who fought, not just with metal, but with magic too. This is the story of their arrival in Ireland, and how they conquered the Fir Bolg to make it their home.*

Nuada, king of the Tuatha Dé Danann – the people of the goddess Danu – stared out over his palace balcony, but he was not looking at the beautiful red rooftops of his beloved city of Murias. Instead, he was watching the hulking volcano which towered over his home. For centuries, it had lain dormant, the perfect backdrop to the royal city. But in recent years it had awoken, spitting angry clouds of black smoke into the sky, and now it rumbled like thunder.

As he often did when he was worried, Nuada rubbed the sun-wheel design on the breastplate of his armour.

"We cannot stay here any longer," he said to the god of healing, Dian Cecht. "Round up the rest of the gods. We must leave at first light."

Dian Cecht bowed and left to send word to the others whilst Nuada went to tell the Dagda, the god of life and death, the news. The Dagda nodded sombrely, gathered his robes around him, and fetched the four things that mattered most to him. First, his magic staff, one end of which was used for bringing death, the other for giving life. Next, he fetched his enchanted harp which could control men's emotions and change the seasons. Then, he took his magic cauldron which never ran out of food.

His greatest treasure he left until the end, for this was his wife, Morrigan, the goddess of war, and he wasn't sure how she'd take the news. He went to the window and whistled into the sky. Seconds later, a crow lit on the sill and hopped down on to the floor.

Before the two men, the bird transformed into a woman with hair as dark as her feathers had been moments earlier, and eyes as black and shining as the bird's. Morrigan was the most feared of all the gods. Her glowing eyes could see into the future and it was well known that if she washed blood off a warrior's armour, that warrior would die in battle.

"What is it, dear husband?" Morrigan asked the Dagda, though she never took her eyes off the king.

She probably knows already, thought Nuada.

And indeed, when the Dagda told her, she didn't seem surprised. Instead, she stared at the king's armour, her eyes turning white.

"What's wrong, Morrigan?" asked Nuada.

"Blood," she said, pointing at his arm. "There's blood on your armour."

When Nuada looked down he saw that there were indeed three drops of blood on the plate covering his arm, though his arm itself was not bleeding. Morrigan wiped the drops away with the corner of her shawl, making Nuada's knees go weak. Did Morrigan cleaning his blood away mean that something terrible would befall him on the journey he was about to take?

Nuada didn't sleep that night. Had Morrigan's vision been an omen of his death? Was this voyage away from their home a foolish idea?

So it was with a heavy heart that Nuada went down to the quay the next morning, where the other gods waited for him. Among them was Oghma, who had invented writing, and Goibniu, who could create anything out of metal. They carried with them the four treasures of the Tuatha Dé Danann: the Dagda's cauldron, the Lia Fáil (Stone of Destiny) which would scream when a true king touched it, a spear which never missed its mark, and the magic Sword of Light.

"Hurry up, you gods!" came a voice on the wind.

Everyone looked up to where the god of the sea, Manannán, stood at the bow of his huge ship, *Wave Sweeper.* The fish-scale skin on his arms rippled iridescent as he tugged on the reins of Enbarr, the horse that would pull them across the ocean.

Nuada and the gods joined the thousands of druids, craftsmen and soldiers already on board, and they set off in search of a new world, leaving their beautiful cities and a smoking volcano behind.

Enbarr galloped through the waves, pulling the great ship behind him. For weeks they travelled, without seeing land, and Nuada began to worry that he was leading his people to their deaths.

One day, the Dagda came running to tell him that Morrigan had a vision of land ahead.

"Well, that's good news, isn't it?" said the king.

"There's more to it than that," said the Dagda. "Come."

Nuada went with the Dagda to the middle of the deck where a crowd had gathered around Morrigan, who was in a stupor, her eyes turned white. Nobody spoke until she came out of her trance, and her eyes returned to their normal black.

"What did you see?" asked Nuada.

"To be sure, there is land ahead," she said, "but it is one of great magic, and its waters are guarded by terrible giants called the Fomorians who will crush our ship with their bare hands."

Fearful of these giants, the gods conferred for a long time, before Nuada finally said, "If we can't go through the waters to reach land, let us go above them," and he explained his plan.

The gods and their most powerful druids gathered in a circle on the deck, and channelled their energy and magic into the centre, while chanting ancient incantations that only the Tuatha Dé Danann knew. At first, a tiny wisp of smoke appeared, but as the magic words grew louder, the smoke curled to produce more, until a white cloud floated inside the circle of magicians. Then it spread out and flowed between their legs, sliding across the deck like snakes, and over the sides.

The magic mist enveloped the ship, tugging it free from the waters and pulling it into the air. Higher and higher it rose, until birds flew beneath their prow.

The gods gazed down at the sea beneath and caught their first glimpse of the emerald isle that would become their new home. The Fomorian giants patrolling the island's shore knew nothing of what was hidden in the clouds, passing over their heads.

When they found a nice green plain, they used their magic to guide the *Wave Sweeper* down on to land.

Nuada marvelled at the beauty of the new country, and smiled his first smile in weeks. He had made the right decision.

"I name this new land 'Inis Fáil', Island of Destiny," said Nuada, marvelling at its natural beauty. "Because it was destiny that brought us here, and here we shall remain until the end of our days."

Everyone agreed, and as a sign that they planned never to leave, they burned their ship.

But little did the Tuatha Dé Danann know they were not welcome in Ireland. A different people, the Fir Bolg, had already made it their home and weren't prepared to share it.

On hearing of the Tuatha Dé Danann's arrival, King Eochaid of the Fir Bolg sent Sreng, his best fighter, to meet the newcomers. As Sreng approached the Tuatha Dé Danann settlement, Nuada sent out his own champion, Bres, to meet him.

"We come in peace," said Bres, "as long as you can make space for us in your country. Give us half your land to live on. Refuse, and you shall feel the wrath of the Tuatha Dé Danann."

Sreng took the message back to his king, who was infuriated at the idea of giving up half his land, and gathered his troops about him.

As Nuada waited for a reply from Sreng, he noticed a dark shape in the sky. A crow.

The bird fluttered to the ground at his feet and

transformed into Morrigan.

"I have flown from the hill of their high king," she said, "and from there, he marches with an army in this direction."

"Then there is no time to waste," replied Nuada. "We must ready ourselves for war."

Morrigan smiled, and in a flutter of dark feathers, took to the sky.

The two armies met and a great battle took place. Shield and sword clashed with a deafening clamour, and the sky was darkened by slingshot and spear.

Even though he was king, Nuada could not stand by and watch his people being slaughtered. With a battle cry of fury, he leaped over fallen warriors, and came face to face with Sreng. However, the king was no match for Sreng's sword, which sliced the air at lightning speed and cut Nuada's arm clean off.

Enraged by their king's injury, the Tuatha Dé Danann pushed Sreng back and quickly brought the bleeding leader to Dian Cecht, their god of healing.

The healer frowned at the place where Nuada's arm had once been, and then ordered Goibniu, the smith, to fetch his finest silver.

"The king needs medicine, not riches," complained Goibniu.

"Just go!" shouted Dian Cecht.

Almost unconscious, Nuada remembered how Morrigan had cleaned blood off his arm plate, and now he understood her prophecy. She had foreseen this injury. Had she foreseen his death as well?

Goibniu returned with silver, and for hours Dian Cecht worked his dark magic on it, chanting incantations as old as the world. By morning, Nuada was back on his feet with a magical arm made of silver. He returned to the battlefield, stronger than ever, a warrior king, half flesh and bone, half metal. From that day on he would be known as Nuada of the Silver Arm.

Even though they'd lost their king, the Fir Bolg fought on bravely, but after four days, the Tuatha Dé Danann got the upper hand and drove the Fir Bolg out of the country.

Nuada took residence in the king's settlement in Tara, bringing with him the Lia Fáil or Stone of Destiny, and planting it on the hill. When he placed his hand upon it, the stone screamed out, proclaiming him the rightful king of Ireland.

The Lia Fáil still stands on Tara today, waiting for the next true king to touch it.

Balor of the Evil Eye

Ireland's oldest myths come from the Lebor Gabála Érenn *or the "Book of Invasions" which chronicles the arrival of six groups of people to Ireland, and how each group had to fight off a ferocious race of sea giants called the Fomorians. This is the story of the Fomorian king who had to learn the dangers of too much power and greed the hard way.*

The king of the Fomorions was called Balor of the Evil Eye, a giant, as tall as a tree, with one eye ten times larger than the other. This massive eye had an ivory ring pierced through its eyelid, and a set of pulleys mounted on the eyebrow.

He didn't always have a huge eye. When he was small, (although in this case, "small" means twice the size of a tall man, because Balor was a Fomorian, after all – the son of a giant mother and a giant father) he had two perfectly normal-sized eyes. But all this changed when, one day, Balor was snooping around the Temple of Alchemy, a place where the Fomorian magicians brewed up spells for use against their enemies. The young boy knew the place was out of bounds, but having heard stories of the magic that happened there, Balor knew he had to see what went on inside. He crept quietly to an open window and peered in. Within, he saw a circle of robed magicians known as druids, chanting dark words over a cauldron bubbling with toxic fumes. But just as he leaned in, a wisp of the poisonous smoke escaped the cauldron and drifted towards the open window, straight into Balor's eye. Immediately, Balor fell to the ground, screaming in pain and clutching at his face. The commotion brought the druids rushing outside to see what all the noise was about. With horror, they explained to Balor that they had been concocting a death spell and the fumes of it had brought the power of death to Balor's eye. Anybody he would look at with that cursed eye would die immediately, so the druids told him he should keep it tightly closed forever.

Balor, however, didn't think he was cursed. He was excited about his new ability and wanted to test it out. So he found a remote part of the island, and opened his eye to look at a passing flock of birds. The creatures fell from the sky like stones.

To Balor, his eye wasn't a curse, but a gift – a gift that would one day make him the most powerful Fomorian that ever lived.

As he got older, Balor's eye grew abnormally large, making it difficult to move about, but he eventually got used to it. Soon, however, the enormous eyelid became too heavy to open without help. An ivory ring was driven through it and pulleys were mounted on his eyebrow. Using ropes, it took ten men to open the eyelid, but when the eye was open, ten times that number could be killed with a single look. Balor didn't open it often, but when he did, his enemies ran from him without a backward glance.

Balor's power meant that he grew up to be the most feared giant among the Fomorians, and they soon made him king, building him a glass tower on Tory Island, from which he could spot passing ships and send his pirate warriors out to raid them.

For a while, Balor was content, but then one of his druids brought terrible news. In a dream, he had witnessed Balor's death.

"You will die at the hand of your grandson," said the druid.

Determined to escape this fate, Balor said, "Then I must ensure I never have grandchildren."

He locked his only child, Eithlinn, in another tower on Tory Island, providing her with twelve handmaidens to guard her. He warned them never to let her set eyes on a man or even mention a man in her presence, thinking that if she only ever had contact with women she would never have a child.

When the Tuatha Dé Danann, wondrous beings with magical powers and gifts, made Ireland their home, Balor was annoyed that they had got past his pirate patrols.

"How did this happen?" he bellowed at his men.

"They used magic to fly their ship over our heads," one of them replied.

"Magic, you say?"

"Oh yes, they have all sorts of magical things, like a cauldron that never runs out of food and a magic cow."

"A magic cow?" Balor liked cows.

"Yes. It has white and green spots and never runs out of milk."

Balor smiled. He fancied a cow like that, and whatever Balor wanted, Balor took.

He had one of his druids disguise him as a red-headed human boy and headed inland. There, he found a strong man called Cian, minding the magical cow outside Goibniu's forge. In his human child disguise, Balor could never overpower the man. He'd have to come up with some other way. An idea came to him.

"Are you waiting to have a sword made?" asked Balor.

"As soon as my brother comes out," replied Cian, petting the cow.

"I bet your brother is taking the best metal, and there'll be none left for you," said Balor.

Worried that this might be the case, Cian rushed

inside, leaving the magic cow behind. Dragging the animal after him, Balor took the cow back to Tory Island, laughing the whole way.

Cian was furious when he realized he'd been tricked by Balor, but he'd heard all about the evil eye, and couldn't simply turn up at Tory Island to retrieve his animal for fear he would be killed.

Instead, he went to a druid called Biróg for help.

"Where does this Balor live?" she asked, agreeing to help him best the evil giant.

"In a tower on Tory Island," said Cian.

She disguised Cian as a woman and conjured up a powerful wind to take herself and Cian to the island. The wind carried them across the sea. What they didn't know was that there were two towers on Tory, one where Balor lived, and one containing his daughter, Eithlinn. It was Eithlinn's tower that they saw first, and presuming it to be Balor's, the druid commanded the wind to deposit them at its door.

"It's getting dark," Biróg called at the door. "Please take pity on two women travellers."

Eithlinn's handmaidens granted Cian and Biróg entry to the tower. Thinking that they were guards, Biróg put a sleeping spell on the handmaidens. Cian threw off his disguise, drew his sword and rushed to the top of the tower to confront Balor. However, he found neither king nor cow. Instead he found Eithlinn, the most beautiful woman he'd ever seen. The pair fell madly in love.

Cian wanted to take Eithlinn back to the mainland with him, but Biróg, terrified of what Balor's revenge might be, convinced Cian to leave her behind. She summoned another enchanted wind and spirited herself and the reluctant Cian back to Ireland.

Of course, Eithlinn was heartbroken that Cian had left, but her sorrow was eased a little when she discovered she was pregnant with his child. A few months later, she gave birth to a boy called Lugh.

Eithlinn pleaded with her handmaidens, who had helped deliver the baby, not to tell Balor the news, but out of fear, one of them did. Knowing that this child could fulfil the prophecy of his death, Balor ordered the baby to be drowned. Lugh was thrown into the sea, leaving Balor content that he no longer had a grandchild that could kill him.

However, the baby did not drown, for it was snatched from the sea by Biróg, who had been riding the winds. She brought the baby back to Cian, who was overjoyed to be united with his son. Cian raised the boy himself, teaching Lugh the arts of metalwork, woodwork, poetry, music, medicine, magic and war. So skilful did he become with a spear that he became known as Lugh of the Long Arm.

Meanwhile, the Tuatha Dé Danann grew prosperous in Ireland, and this infuriated Balor. He demanded they pay him a tax or he'd declare war. King Nuada laughed at these demands and Balor had no choice but to go to war in order to keep his promise. He assembled a huge army to go to battle against the Tuatha Dé Danann.

Back in Tara, King Nuada knew nothing of Balor's preparations, and was enjoying a meal, when a man arrived at the door. A strange, magical light shone from his face and long golden hair, and his armour too, seemed to glow.

"Who are you?" asked the doorkeepers.

"I am Lugh of the Long Arm," said the warrior. "I want to join the king's household."

"What special skill do you bring with you?" asked the doorkeepers.

"I do not bring one—"

"Then you will not be allowed in," interrupted one of the doorkeepers, "for everybody in Nuada's household has a special skill."

"I wasn't finished speaking," said Lugh. "I do not bring just one skill – I bring them all, for I am a master of carpentry, metalwork, music, fighting, poetry, magic and healing."

When the king heard Lugh's boast, he was disbelieving, but allowed Lugh entry to find out whether he had the talents he spoke of. And so Lugh played chess against everyone in the king's court and beat them all. He lifted a boulder that no other man could lift, and played such beautiful music on the harp that the king cried.

Nuada welcomed Lugh into his household, and the timing could not have been better, because just then, a messenger arrived with news of the Fomorian army marching towards Tara, led by Balor.

"Lugh of the Long Arm," said Nuada. "You shall be commander of my army, and together we shall take down these monsters."

The Tuatha Dé Danann assembled their greatest army and set out to meet the advancing Fomorians. As was customary, the kings, commanders and other leaders hung back while the ordinary soldiers fought.

Fired up for battle by Lugh's encouragement, the

Tuatha Dé Danann fought bravely and fiercely, but were no match for the Fomorian giants. However, no matter how bedraggled and worn the soldiers were, at the end of each day, the Tuatha Dé Danann's wounded were cured by their druids and physicians and sent back fresh for action the following day. But after days of fighting, the Fomorians had gained the upper hand and the spirits of the Tuatha army were flagging.

"I cannot stand by and watch any longer," said Lugh to Nuada and, grabbing a spear, he joined the fray. King Nuada, along with his champions and gods, followed. Spurred on by the sight of their heroes, the Tuatha pushed the Fomorians back to where Balor waited.

Enraged by the sight of his retreating army, Balor leaped into battle, swinging a sword the size of a small tree. Scores of Tuatha fell under each stroke, including the great king, Nuada himself.

At the sight of his king dying at Balor's feet, Lugh leaped forward and challenged the grandfather that had tried to drown him as a baby.

"Open that ugly eye and show us what it can do!" screamed Lugh.

"Who is this mouse that squeaks at me?" laughed Balor.

"This mouse goes by the name of Lugh of the Long Arm. I am the son of Cian and Eithlinn. I am your grandson."

Balor dropped his sword, and the colour drained from his face. "What. . ."

"What am I doing here?" shouted Lugh. "I'm here to fulfil the prophecy of your death."

Balor blinked away the shock that had momentarily stunned him into inaction.

"Open my eye!" he commanded.

His men tied ropes to the ivory ring in his eyelid. These ropes were then threaded through the pulleys which were mounted on his eyebrow. Ten Fomorian giants pulled with all their strength on the ropes until slowly the eyelid began to open.

Balor's evil eye scanned the battlefield, felling waves of Tuatha soldiers with its death stare. Skilled as he was, Lugh knew he couldn't escape. He had to act fast.

Quickly, he put a stone in his sling, and flung it hard at the eye, just as its gaze was upon him. The stone hit Balor so hard that it drove the eye back into his head and out the other side, landing among the Fomorians, and killing those nearby.

Balor crumpled to the ground with such force that

the whole battlefield shook. With their leader now dead, the Fomorians lost heart and retreated back to the sea, leaving the Tuatha Dé Danann to celebrate their victory. And so the prophecy of Balor's death was fulfilled. The evil king of the giants was killed by his own grandchild.

Lugh of the Long Arm was celebrated all over Ireland for his bravery, soon becoming the new High King of Ireland and leading Ireland with strength and courage for the rest of his days.

The Children of Lir

"The Children of Lir" is probably the best-known story in this book. Almost every school child in Ireland is familiar with it. Over the years, the tale has inspired countless artists. A famous sculpture called "The Children of Lir" by Oisín Kelly can be seen in the Garden of Remembrance in Dublin.

Lir, a wealthy chieftain, was married to the king's daughter, Eve, who he loved with all his heart. They had four beautiful children: Fionnuala – the eldest; her brother – Aodh, whose hair was as red as fire; and the twin boys, Conn and Fiachra. They all lived happily in Lir's hilltop fort.

Disaster struck when Eve died, and though Lir was overcome with grief, his love for his children strengthened. He became so protective of them that he even slept in the same room as them.

Bodb Dearg, or Bov the Red, the children's grandfather, was king of the Tuatha Dé Danann and also a druid, skilled in the practice of magic. He loved his grandchildren almost as much as Lir did. It saddened him to see the children without a mother, so he suggested that Lir marry one of his other daughters, Aoife. What nobody knew, was that Aoife was secretly a witch, and had been training in the arts of dark magic with her father's druids for some time.

Lir and Aoife married, and for a while they were happy, but Aoife soon became jealous of her husband's love for his children. She thought he loved them more than her and jealousy took root in Aoife's soul, becoming a black, evil weed that poisoned her heart. The only solution, in her mind, was to get rid of the children.

"Let's go visit your grandfather," she said, one day when Lir was away.

The twins squealed in delight because they loved visiting the king. Fionnuala, however, was nervous, because she had had a dream that something bad would happen if they left their home. She tried to get out of going, but Aoife insisted.

On their way to the king's fort, Aoife stopped the chariots so that the children could pick flowers for their grandfather. As soon as they were out of earshot, Aoife ordered her men to kill the children. Though the men were battle-hardened warriors, they were not monsters, and refused Aoife's request. Angered by their disobedience, she sent them home, swearing she'd do the job herself.

As Lir's family continued onwards towards the king's fort, a new idea formed in Aoife's mind. She stopped the chariots at Lake Derravaragh, the Lake of Oaks, and asked the children if they'd like a swim to cool down on such a hot day. The younger children jumped at the chance and ran, whooping, into the water. Fionnuala, though she had an uneasy feeling in her stomach, joined them, because she didn't want to leave her brothers alone with Aoife.

When all four children were in the lake, Aoife produced a druid's wand and began chanting dark and ancient words of enchantment. As the spell drifted across the water towards the children, the four felt their bodies change. They screamed as their toes webbed together, and white quills sprouted from their skin. Their necks lengthened and their mouths solidified into hard bills. They had become swans!

Fionnuala swam to the shore and, finding she could still speak, she asked, "Aoife, what have you done?"

"Something I should have done long ago," replied the sorceress. "No longer will I have to share Lir's love with his children. Now it will all be mine."

"Witch!" hissed Fionnuala. "Our father will always love us, even if we're not there. Surely you can't be so cruel as to leave us like this forever."

"Not forever, my child. Just for nine hundred years." Aoife laughed a high-pitched cackle that echoed across the lake. "For the first three hundred years you will stay here. The next three hundred are to be spent on the Sea of Moyle, and the final three hundred on the Sea of Erris. The spell will only be broken when a king from the North marries a queen from the South, and you hear the bell of a new religion ringing."

"But we never did anything to hurt you!" cried Fionnuala. "Please have mercy on us."

Aoife thought for a moment and then nodded. "Here is my mercy. I grant you the gift of song. When you sing, your music shall be like nothing ever heard in the world before. It will lift the hearts of men, and keep you company in your exile."

And with a twirl of her cloak, Aoife disappeared back to her chariot. When she arrived at her father's fort, the king asked her why she hadn't brought Lir's children with her. Aoife, of course, had a story ready.

"It is because Lir knows how much you love his children and he thinks you might steal them away from him."

Now, Bodb Dearg knew Lir well enough to know that Aoife was lying, so he sent his servant to Lir, inviting him to visit, and to bring his children.

When Lir received the message, he said to the

messenger, "Are my children not there already, with Aoife?"

"Aoife is there," replied the messenger, "but not your children."

Lir knew then, that something terrible had happened, and set out immediately for the king's fort. As they passed Lake Derravaragh, Fionnuala saw her father and called out to him. At the sound of his daughter's voice, he stopped the horses, and though he looked around, all he could see were four swans at the edge of the lake.

"It is your daughter, Fionnuala," called the nearest swan. "And your three boys: Aodh, Conn and Fiachra."

Lir was shocked at what he was hearing and raced down to the water's edge, where Fionnuala told him what had happened.

He was heartbroken at the sight of his four beautiful children turned into swans.

"Come home with me, at least," he said, "where I can take care of you."

Fionnuala shook her head. "The spell won't permit us to leave for three hundred years."

Her father lay down on the ground and wept, until he heard the most beautiful music. It brought joy into his grief-stricken heart and, when he looked up to see where it was coming from, he realized the four swans were singing.

The children continued to sing until all the men were lulled into a peaceful sleep. In the morning, Lir set out for Bodb Dearg's fort to find Aoife.

When the king found out what Aoife had done to his grandchildren, he was so enraged that he produced his druidic wand. When he pointed it at his daughter, a fierce wind lifted her up into the air, like a leaf. Screaming, she was carried away into the sky, never to return.

Lir and Bodb Dearg returned to the lake and spent the day talking to the swans, and the night listening to their enchanting music. In fact, the two men never left. They set up camp by the water's edge, and over time, people came from all over Ireland to visit the children of Lir. Those who were ill or unhappy went away cured and at peace. The swans' singing granted good health and long life to Lir and Bodb Dearg, for they passed the ages of one hundred, then two hundred, then three hundred years of age.

Fionnuala knew when the time had come to leave Lake Derravaragh. "My precious brothers, this is our last night in this place, for tomorrow we must leave for the Sea of Moyle."

That night, the king and Lir held a great banquet by the water's edge with fine food. In the morning, the children bade farewell to their beloved father and grandfather.

"We will love you forever," said Lir, with tears in his eyes. "And you will never be forgotten, not until the end of time."

As the sun rose over the twinkling waters of Lake Derravaragh, four majestic swans took to the air, the clapping of their great wings sounding like the heartbeat of Ireland itself. Two very old men watched them disappear into the clouds, before returning back to their homes. The first thing the king did was introduce a law, making it forbidden to harm a swan. A law which still stands to this day in Ireland. The four swans flew north to the Sea of Moyle, a stretch of water between Ireland and Scotland, and it was as different from Lake Derravaragh as you can imagine.

Instead of a sheltered lake, the waters were violent and cold. Every spring, the swans were tossed about on stormy waves. Lightning split the sky in two, and howling winds churned the sea into waves as high as trees, dashing the children against the rocks. On many occasions they nearly lost their lives, but

Fionnuala fought hard to keep her brothers alive. On Carrignarone, the Rock of Seals, she sheltered her brothers under her wings, waiting for spring to pass.

The weather in summer and autumn was a little bit kinder, giving the Lir children more time to dwell on their loneliness, for nobody ever came to the shore to speak to them or listen to their singing.

Winter brought with it freezing gales of sleet, snow and ice. Fionnuala and her three brothers shivered on Carrignarone, and their feet and the tips of their wings sometimes froze fast to the rock. It was a long three hundred years, and when the time was up, the children were glad to leave.

On their flight west towards the Sea of Erris, they decided to fly over their father's fort, but were shocked to find it derelict and overgrown with weeds. Continuing onwards, they discovered the fort of their grandfather, the king, to be the same. What the children didn't know was that the Tuatha Dé Danann had been driven underground and were now nothing but legends. The children of Lir themselves had also become the stuff of stories.

They found the Sea of Erris to be a more tranquil place than Moyle, for they could shelter in the many inlets and islands off the Mayo coast. Their favourite place was a lake on the island of Inisglora, for it reminded them of Derravaragh. Each day, the four swan-children sang their melodic songs to keep away the loneliness. Their music may not have attracted people, but it did bring hundreds of species of bird from the nearby islands of Achill and Aran. Later, the place became known as the Lake of the Birds.

During this time, a new religion had been brought to Ireland by Saint Patrick. The old gods had been replaced by a new one, and his followers sought out isolated places to pray. One day, a holy man came to the island on the Lake of Birds. From the reeds, the children of Lir watched him begin to build a stone church and pray. Desperate for human company, they sang out to him.

He stopped mid-prayer, and rushed down to the water's edge to see four swans approaching.

"The children of Lir," he gasped, for like everyone else, he had heard the legend.

He wasn't surprised when they spoke back to him. They told him their story, and he in turn told them stories about his god. Every day, the monk prayed, worked on his church and chatted to the swans. They lulled him to sleep at night with their singing.

While all this was going on, Lairgren, the king of Connacht, went south to Munster to marry a princess. Of course, the children of Lir didn't know this. Nor did they know that Aoife's prophecy was almost fulfilled: "The spell will only be broken when a king from the North marries a queen from the South, and you hear the bell of a new religion ringing."

Back on the island on the Lake of Birds, the monk had finished building his church. The final touch was the hanging of a large bronze bell. When it was installed, the children of Lir watched their new friend ring it for the first time.

The strange sound rippled across the water, bringing about a curious change in the swans. They felt their skin tighten and their feathers fall away. The boys panicked, but Fionnuala knew what was happening. The nine hundred years were up, and the ringing bell of a new religion had broken Aoife's spell.

"Quickly, on to the land," she told her brothers.

By the time the swans came out of the water, all their feathers had gone. Their webbed feet grew toenails, their wings became arms, their necks shortened, their beaks became mouths, and on their heads sprouted human hair. But it was not the thick, vivid hair of their youth – it was limp and grey.

After nine hundred years, the children of Lir were no longer children, but old people. Frail and wrinkled, they lay on the ground, without the energy to stand.

The monk rushed down to them and knelt beside Fionnuala, who knew she was going to die.

"We are dying, my friend," she said. "Please will you tell us one of your stories as we rest, and bury us in this place where we found peace."

Using the water from the lake to mop their brows, the monk made Lir's children comfortable, and told them stories as they died. Then he buried them in a single grave with Fionnuala's arms around her brothers, just as she had sheltered them with her wings for nine hundred years. The siblings were finally at peace.

The Ulster Cycle

Legends are very similar to myths but are about humans rather than gods. These humans were often brave warriors or leaders. The Ulster Cycle stories are set around the first century during the reign of King Conor Mac Nessa. Most of these legends are about the warrior Cúchulainn.

The Hound of Cullan

When the Milesians (the Celts) came to Ireland, they drove the god-like Tuatha Dé Danann underground into the many fairy mounds dotted across the country. The Tuatha became known as the Sídhe (pronounced shee) or fairies, and though they no longer ruled the land, they became a feared presence in Irish people's lives for thousands of years. This is the story of a gift the Sídhe gave to Ireland, a baby that would grow up to be the country's greatest hero.

Many years before our story starts, King Conor of Ulster woke up to discover that his sister, Dectera, and fifty other girls had disappeared without trace from the royal fort. For years, the king's men searched for them, but the girls were nowhere to be found. As no one could find hide nor hair of them, rumours spread that the girls had been snatched by the fairy Sídhe and taken to the Land of Youth, or Tír na nÓg as it was called in the Irish tongue, never to be seen again...

But one day, while hunting in the forest for birds, Fergus Mac Roy, one of the king's most-trusted men, saw a light coming from a fairy mound. This was most unusual, for the doors to these mounds normally never opened for mortal men.

Stepping inside, Fergus realized that the light was not coming from the mound itself, but from a man with long, golden hair. Fergus knew it was the Tuatha Dé Danann god, Lugh of the Long Arm. Beside him stood a woman that Fergus recognized – Dectera, the king's missing sister. She looked as young as the day she'd gone missing, even though many years had passed.

Fergus immediately wanted to take Dectera back to the king, but she refused to go, explaining how happy she was with Lugh in Tír na nÓg.

"My life won't be worth living if I return to the king empty-handed," said Fergus. "He misses you sorely."

"Then take my child to comfort my brother," she said, handing Fergus a baby, "and raise him well, for he shall be the greatest warrior Ireland has ever known."

The baby was taken back to Ulster amid much celebration. Everyone argued about who should care for the royal child. In the end, King Conor decided the job should go to Dectera's sister, but everybody should have a hand in his rearing, because if he was to be the greatest of warriors he should have the greatest of care. Indeed, the king himself was a regular presence in the child's life. The boy was given the name Setanta.

Even at the age of six, Setanta had the makings of a great warrior, as his mother had predicted. Knowing that he needed training in order to hone his skills, the king invited Setanta to his fort to audition for his troop of trainee soldiers, the Red Branch Knights.

"What if I don't get in?" Setanta asked his foster

mother.

She kissed his forehead. "Just show them how brave and strong you are."

He took a hurley stick and his sliotar (the special ball needed for hurling), a spear and his toy shield, and set off on the journey. He passed the time by hitting the sliotar a great distance into the sky, and launching his spear after it. He would then run ahead and catch, first the sliotar, and then the spear, before they hit the ground.

When Setanta arrived at the king's fort, he found the Red Branch boys playing a game of hurling on the green. Never one to pass an opportunity, Setanta rushed headlong into the game, taking the ball past one player, and then another, before scoring a goal.

The boys, who were much older than Setanta, weren't impressed by this little stranger joining their game uninvited. They belted their sliotars at him, but he batted them away with his hurley. Next, they launched their spears at him, but he deflected these with his shield. Finally, they attacked him with their fists.

The young Setanta's face distorted with anger, his eyes rolling in his head and his teeth bared like a dog. A strange light radiated from his head. The boys did not know this, but what they were witnessing was the light of the god, Lugh, Setanta's father, shining out of him. They were so shocked by the sight that they were unprepared for Setanta's attack. He rushed at the boys, knocking twenty of them to the ground.

When the king heard about the fearless newcomer, he knew it could only be one person – Setanta – and he invited him to join the boys' troop of the Red Branch Knights.

"What about my audition?" asked Setanta.

The king laughed, and pointed at the twenty abashed boys. "You've just done it. And passed."

For the next few months, Setanta was trained in the disciplines of poetry, music, fitness and fighting, and indeed proved himself to be champion of them all. He soon became leader of the troop and a favourite of the king – quite an achievement for a seven-year-old.

So much so, that when King Conor was invited to the feast of a blacksmith called Cullan, he asked Setanta to come along as a guest. This was a big honour for Setanta because Cullan was renowned as one of the finest makers of weapons in the entire land.

However, when the time came to depart for Cullan's fort, Setanta was in the middle of a game of hurling, and didn't want to leave before it was finished.

"I'll follow when the game is over," he told the king.

Conor, who normally wouldn't have accepted this insolence from anyone, was charmed by the boy's dedication to the game. He smiled, nodded, and set off in his chariot.

After the game of hurling which, unsurprisingly, Setanta's team won, the boy headed off in the direction of Cullan's fort. He passed the time by hitting his sliotar into the sky and then running ahead to catch it.

Meanwhile, at Cullan's fort, King Conor arrived with his men and was invited inside to a magnificent feast of fresh boar meat and badger flesh roasted in honey, and the finest of wine served in silver goblets made by Cullan himself.

"Who guards your fort while we feast?" asked the king.

"I have no need of soldiers," replied Cullan, "for I have the best guard dog in the country – a wolfhound as large as a bear and as fierce as a wolf."

The king laughed, and tucked into more food, forgetting that Setanta was on his way.

Outside Cullan's fort, his wolfhound prowled,

a beast of sharp eyes, cocked ears and dagger-like teeth.

It was almost dark by the time Setanta reached Cullan's fort. From inside, he could hear the music, chatter and laughter of the banquet, but he could hear another noise too. A low, threatening growl, like the rumble of thunder rolled across the grass in front of the gate.

From out of the shadows, pounced the biggest Irish wolfhound the boy had ever seen. It was the same height as Setanta himself. Its eyes seemed to burn red with fire, and drool flew from its bared fangs as it bounded across the open space towards him.

With no time to run away, Setanta lifted his hurley and, pulling his arm back, drove his sliotar with all his might at the attacking beast. The ball whistled through the air like an arrow, flying straight into the hound's open mouth. With an ear-piercing squeal, the dog dropped dead to the ground.

Cullan, the king, and all the guests rushed outside to see what had made such an infernal noise. In the moonlight, they saw the seven-year-old Setanta, hurley in hand, standing over the lifeless body of Cullan's hound.

The king, who had forgotten that Setanta would be

arriving late, was relieved to see the boy unharmed. Cullan, on the other hand, was distraught at the loss of his prized guard dog.

"Who will protect my family now?" he said, running his fingers through the dead animal's fur.

"Find me a pup of the same breed," said Setanta, "and I will raise him to be your guard dog. And until he is old enough to protect you and your family, I will guard your fort. I will be the hound of Cullan."

The king, impressed by the boy's courage and generosity, asked if Cullan was happy with this arrangement. The smith said he was, and from that day, Setanta became known by his new name – Cúchulainn, the Hound of Cullan.

Cúchulainn and Emer

With a mother who was the king's sister and a father who was a Tuatha Dé Danann god, Cúchulainn grew up to be the finest warrior in Ulster (one of the provinces of Ireland). He was a respected member of King Conor's Red Branch Knights. Nobody could match his skills in sword and spear play, juggling, tight-rope walking and chess. He was wise and kind, except when the battle fury came over him and he turned into a raging, unstoppable warrior, but that was a rare occurrence. This is the story of how he fell in love and found his wife.

Cúchulainn had long, dark hair, a finely toned body, and the most handsome face in the king's court. It was no wonder that all the women who set eyes on him fell madly in love. Cúchulainn, however, had no interest in getting married. That is, until he laid eyes on Emer the Fair at a banquet.

Her skin was as white as milk and her eyes sparkled green and amber like those of a hawk. Her golden hair was styled into long braids, at the end of which hung red and silver balls which swung when she moved between the guests. She was the most beautiful woman Cúchulainn had ever seen, and he instantly knew that she was to be his wife.

He told her he wanted to marry her, but she laughed at him.

"You are but a boy," she said. "My father will only allow me to marry a champion."

"Then that is what I will become," said Cúchulainn. "I will return when I am not just a champion, but the greatest champion there ever was."

When he arrived home he asked every man in his uncle's fort how he would become such a champion.

"You are already one," they told him.

"But I want to become the best champion in all of Ireland. I need to prove that I am worthy of Emer's hand in marriage," said Cúchulainn.

His questions eventually brought him to the table of the king.

"The greatest champions," said Conor Mac Nessa, "train with the woman warrior, Scathach, the Shadowy One. Only she can teach you the secrets of war and weaponry."

"Great," said Cúchulainn. "Where can I find her?"

The king laughed. "That is part of the challenge, my boy, for nobody knows where she lives. They say that only those who are truly deserving will find her."

Determined to be one of the truly deserving, Cúchulainn scoured the length and breadth of Ireland asking about Scathach's whereabouts but, though many had heard of her, nobody knew where she lived.

He was about to give up when he came across an old man, sitting by the sea.

He pointed a feeble finger across the ocean towards Scotland. "The place you seek is the Land of Shadows, but the road there is full of danger, and though some have travelled it, most have not returned."

Undeterred, Cúchulainn pressed the man for more specific directions.

"I can guide you as far as the Plain of Ill Luck," said the man. "After that, you're on your own."

"Why is it called the Plain of Ill Luck?"

"Because the first part of the plain is a treacherous bog, which if you sink into, you'll never escape. The second part contains a meadow with grass so sharp it'll cut your feet to pieces."

Cúchulainn thanked the man, found a boat, and set off for Scotland.

Some days later, he arrived at the Plain of Ill Luck, and was wondering how he'd get through it, when he spotted a man with bright, glowing hair carrying a flaming wheel in one hand and a golden apple in the other.

"I've come to help you," said the stranger. "Roll this wheel over the bog and follow its path. When you reach the meadow, roll this apple through the grass and follow it."

He handed Cúchulainn the apple and the flaming wheel, which strangely didn't burn his skin. Before

Cúchulainn could begin to thank him, the man disappeared into thin air.

What Cúchulainn didn't know was that he had just been visited by his father, the Tuatha Dé Danann god, Lugh of the Long Arm.

Cúchulainn rolled the flaming wheel in front of him and its heat hardened the bog beneath it, creating a firm path to walk on. The wheel led him to a meadow of knife-like grass. He rolled the apple ahead of him, which magically created a safe path, wider than the apple, through the blades.

After the meadow, Cúchulainn came to an inlet, jutting out into the sea. Below, he could hear the waves pounding the cliffs, and sea birds screeching into the wind. At the end of the headland he spied a group of boys playing hurling. Stopping their game when they saw Cúchulainn approach, a tall, fair-haired boy stepped forward and introduced himself as Ferdia of Connacht.

"I'm looking for Scathach and the Land of Shadows," said Cúchulainn.

Ferdia pointed out into the sea at an island of sharp, black rocks. "That is the Land of Shadows, home to Scathach, the Shadowy One, and Queen of Warriors."

"How do I get out to it?"

"You do not. Scathach comes to you. This is why we, her students, are waiting here."

"But how does Scathach cross?"

Ferdia pointed at a narrow bridge. "The Bridge of Leaps can only be crossed in a single bound. It's the last thing Scathach teaches her trainees. Try and cross it any other way, and you'll be flung off."

Cúchulaiin, never one to shirk a challenge, took off his crimson cloak. "I haven't come all this way to sit around waiting for Scathach to come to me. I shall go to her."

The boys watched as Cúchulainn ran for the bridge, but as soon as he put his foot upon it, it reared up and tossed him back on to land. His onlookers couldn't help but laugh.

Now angry, Cúchulainn dusted himself down and ran at the bridge again, this time trying to leap across it. He landed before the halfway point, and again the bridge flipped him back into the crowd of laughing boys.

Cúchulainn was so furious now that his battle fury came upon him. His face reddened, one eye squinting, the other bulging, and shafts of light burst out of his head like a crown.

Flabbergasted into silence, the boys watched Cúchulainn make a third run at the bridge, before propelling himself into the air. This time, he landed on the middle of the bridge and before it had time to flip him off, he leaped again, landing safely on Scathach's island.

The warrior queen, who had been watching Cúchulainn's attempts, strode across the grass to meet him. A hunting dog prowled on either side of her. Tall and lean-faced, she wore a leather tunic and saffron wool kilt. Her bare arms sported bronze jewellery and the white scars of battle.

"I am Cúchulainn, the Hound of Ulster," said the boy. "I've come to learn to be a champion."

Scathach gazed at him with steel-grey eyes. "The first thing you should learn is not to attempt to cross that bridge again, not until I've taught you the Hero's Salmon Leap, because it would be such a shame to lose the best pupil that has ever come to me."

And so, Cúchulainn stayed with Scathach for a year and a day, learning all there was to know about hand-to-hand combat and the craft of war. He learned new weapon techniques, like how to throw a spear with his foot. During that time, he went to battle alongside his teacher in skirmishes with neighbouring tribes, and on many occasions, saved her life.

He also built up a great friendship with Ferdia, even though he was from Connacht, a province often at war with Cuchulainn's Ulster. They became like brothers and promised to always look out for each other.

At the end of his training, Scathach taught Cúchulainn the Hero's Salmon Leap, an enormous jump which allowed him to clear the Bridge of Leaps in a single bound.

As a parting gift, Scathach gave Cúchulainn the Gae Bolg or Belly Spear, which could pierce any armour and never missed its mark.

Though sad to leave, Cúchulainn was excited to see his friends back in Ulster and, of course, Emer the Fair. He felt sure he was now the champion of all the men in Ireland and nothing would stop him from winning her hand in marriage.

But as soon as he arrived home he learned that while he'd been away, Emer's father had promised her hand in marriage to the king of Munster.

"We'll see about that," said Cúchulainn, hopping into his chariot.

Some of his friends followed him in the direction of Emer's fort. When they arrived, they found the gates closed.

"Open up!" shouted Cúchulainn, "for I am the Hound of Ulster, and I've come for my bride."

"Go home, little puppy!" replied Emer's father from inside. "My daughter is promised to another."

"And is this your daughter's wish as well as yours?"

"It is not, but I am her father, and she'll do as I command!"

With that, Cúchulainn stepped out of his chariot and raced towards the gates, building up the power in his strides as he ran. Just as he arrived at the gate, he flung himself into the air in a tremendous Hero's Salmon Leap – one of which Scathach would have been proud.

The Hound of Ulster sailed over the gates and the heads of the armed warriors inside, landing in the middle of the fort, his crimson cloak flapping behind him, and his weapons glinting in the sun.

The warriors of Emer's fort were so stunned by this feat of athleticism that they stared open-mouthed at the intruder.

"What are you gaping at, you fools?" bellowed Emer's father. "Attack!"

They came at him in waves of sword and spear, but Cúchulainn put into action everything that

Scathach had taught him, and mowed his attackers down like corn.

Watching from the women's quarters where her father had her confined, Emer's heart burst with joy at the sight of Cúchulainn. Since he'd proposed to her, he was all she'd been able to think about. She had been horrified and furious when her father had promised her to the king of Munster, a man old enough to be her grandfather, and large enough to be her pig.

Outside the fort, Cúchulainn's friends had lit a fire at the base of the gates, and soon the dry timber was crackling with flames.

When the ground was littered with fallen warriors, Emer raced out into the arms of Cúchulainn, just as a team of chariots burst through the burning gates.

Cúchulainn hoisted Emer on to his shoulder and hopped into his chariot, which swung around in a cloud of dust, and back out the gate.

With Emer's fort now a pyre of smoke and flame behind them, Cúchulainn said, "Am I champion enough for you now?"

Emer laughed, nodded and kissed him.

The wedding lasted seven days and seven nights and would be talked about for years to come, and although they had their bad times as well as good, Cúchulainn and Emer remained married for the rest of their lives.

The Cattle Raid of Cooley

The first half of this epic tale was discovered in an eleventh century manuscript called the Book of the Dun Cow. *The second half was found later on, in the fourteenth century manuscript, the* Yellow Book of Lecan. *However, the story probably existed for hundreds of years before that in oral form.*

Ireland is divided into provinces. Each one used to have its own king or queen who bowed to nobody except the High King of Ireland, who lived in Tara.

In the most northern province, Ulster, a wealthy farmer once bragged that his wife, Macha, was faster than the king's horses. When the king heard this, he told the farmer to prove it. Macha refused to race because she was heavily pregnant, but the king insisted. Macha won the race, but fell to the ground on the finishing line and gave birth to twins. Afterwards, she put a curse on the men of Ulster that they would suffer a terrible weakness in their time of greatest need.

The ruler of Ulster's neighbouring province of Connacht was the tall and fierce Queen Maeve. One day, she was arguing with her husband, Ailill, about which of the pair was the wealthiest. When they counted their possessions, they discovered they had exactly the same amount of land, jewellery, sheep and cattle. In all things they were equal, except one. Ailill owned a magnificent white bull.

Maeve, who was not used to defeat, sent her men

the length and breadth of Ireland in search of a bull that could equal her husband's. They found such an animal on the Cooley Peninsula, which was then part of Ulster – a brown bull whose back was so broad that fifty children could play hurling on it.

Maeve sent her messengers into Ulster to the bull's owner, Daire, asking for a loan of the animal for one year. Daire agreed, and laid on a feast for Maeve's men. While they were celebrating with mead and wine, Daire overheard one of them boasting that if the bull hadn't been given to them, they would have taken it by force. Unsurprisingly, Daire changed his mind about lending the bull to Maeve, and sent the messengers back to Connacht empty-handed. Maeve was furious at being refused, and gathered together all the tribes of Connacht to go to war against Ulster.

Now, luck was on Maeve's side, because many years previously, a curse had been put on the men of Ulster, that they would suffer a terrible weakness in their time of greatest need. When the Ulstermen heard of Maeve's army gathering at their borders, the curse struck them down, turning their legs to liquid and inflicting horrible pains upon them. Women and children were immune, but every man was affected except one Ulsterman – Cúchulainn, for he had the blood of the Tuatha Dé Danann god, Lugh, inside him.

In his chariot, armed with spear and shield, Cúchulainn set off to defend Ulster while her men were recovering from the Great Weakness.

Maeve's army, over five thousand strong, cowered at the sight of the single warrior waiting on the hill, his dark hair and crimson cloak fluttering in the wind. They had heard the stories about the Hound of Ulster. They knew that what they were facing was more than just a man. And if they were in any doubt, the battle fury that came upon Cúchulainn confirmed what they had suspected – that he was half man, half god.

His face contorted and a golden light burst out of his head. Screaming, he charged towards Maeve's army and felled her men by the hundred, cutting a path through them in his chariot, and then turning around to do the same again.

When enough damage had been done, Cúchulainn retreated to a narrow ford and challenged Maeve to send him her best champion each day to fight in single combat. Intent on occupying Ulster and retrieving the Brown Bull of Cooley, Maeve sent champion after champion to fight, but nobody was capable of getting past the Hound of Cullan, except maybe, one man – Ferdia, Cúchulainn's old friend who he'd met in Scathach's training school. However, when all the champions were stepping forward to fight, Ferdia hung back, because he didn't want to fight his best friend.

Maeve hadn't asked him to fight because she knew he'd refuse. Now, she begged him, offering him great herds of cattle, land, and even the hand of her own daughter in marriage, but still he refused.

"You wouldn't like to be the next King of Connacht?" she asked.

"Of course I would," said Ferdia. "But I won't fight Cúchulainn. He's like a brother to me, and we promised to always look out for each other."

Maeve turned away. "If you're too scared to fight, that's fine."

Ferdia, who was a proud warrior, called her back. "I'm not scared of anything."

"That's not what my soldiers say. They say you're no match for Cúchulainn. They even say that the Hound of Ulster claims this himself."

At this, Ferdia's blood boiled in anger and he agreed to fight.

"Nobody calls me a coward," he spat.

The next day, the two men met at the ford, not in a violent clash, but in a firm embrace.

"It's good to see you, my old friend," said Cúchulainn.

"Less of the old," laughed Ferdia, and then more solemnly, said, "You know why I am here?"

Cúchulainn nodded. "It'll be just like when we were training together with Scathach."

"Except this time, it's for real," said Ferdia.

"As you are my guest," said Cúchulainn, "you may choose the weapons."

Ferdia chose the javelins. For the rest of the day each man hurled his weapons at the other, but each spear was either skillfully dodged or caught on a shield. By sundown, not a wound had been inflicted.

That night, the friends shared a meal of roasted rabbit, and slept side by side under the stars.

In the morning, Cúchulainn's weapon of choice was the broad-bladed spear, and for hours the two men fought hand-to-hand, inflicting only minor wounds. At nightfall, they tended to each other's wounds but slept on separate banks of the river.

The next day, Cúchulainn thought Ferdia looked tired and offered him the chance to back down without dishonour.

"I cannot look the men of Connacht in their eyes if

I back down," he said, his voice lacking confidence. "Today, I choose the swords."

The sound of iron on iron rang out across the valley all day. Metal bit into flesh and both men cried out in pain, but by the nightfall, both were still standing. They returned to their camps without speaking or tending to each other's wounds.

When Ferdia woke the next morning he knew this would be his final day of battle, so he dressed in his best armour. He hung a large flat stone under the iron apron over his chest to protect himself from Cúchulainn's belly spear, the Gae Bolg. The weapon, which was fired with the foot, had been a gift to Cúchulainn from their old teacher, Scathach, and Ferdia knew it never missed its mark.

"Your choice of weapon today, Cúchulainn," said Ferdia, fixing the strap of his helmet.

"Today, I choose all weapons," said Cúchulainn.

Ferdia's stomach flipped in fear, for he knew this included the Gae Bolg.

All morning they fought with spears, and by midday, changed to sword and shield, but neither warrior got the better of the other.

Panting with weariness, Cúchulainn lowered his shield to catch a breath. Ferdia saw his chance and thrust his sword forward, catching his opponent on the shoulder. Blood spilling, the Hound of Cullan staggered back towards his own side of the river and grabbed Scathach's belly spear.

Using his foot, he hurled the weapon at Ferdia, who raised his bronze shield to block it, but it was no use. The Gae Bolg flew straight through the shield and pierced Ferdia's iron apron, splitting the stone underneath in two. The spear went straight through Ferdia as well, emerging the other side of his body wet and red. With a cry, he dropped his weapons and fell to his knees in the water. Cúchulainn caught him and dragged him to the riverbank.

With tears in his eyes, he cradled his dying friend and said, "I'm here, Ferdia."

Ferdia gathered the last of his energy to speak.

"You promised to be always at my side, and right at the end, here you are."

Cúchulainn nodded, and one of his tears fell on to his friend's face. It was the last thing Ferdia ever felt.

Meanwhile, the curse of the Great Weakness was wearing off the men of Ulster. The king, Conor Mac Nessa, rose to his feet and steadied himself on his sword.

"We must go to Cúchulainn's aid!" he shouted,

feeling the strength return to his bones.

He summoned every tribe in Ulster to march towards Maeve's armies.

When Ferdia had been slain, Maeve knew none of her other men were a match for Cúchulainn. The terms of their agreement meant that Maeve should have surrendered, but victory was more important to Maeve than honour.

If the Hound wants me to send him champions, she thought, *then champions he shall have. All of them at once!*

She climbed into her chariot and rode out in front of her army. Raising her spear, she screamed, "Attack!"

Though weary from days of fighting, Cúchulainn was not afraid when he saw the Connacht army approach. He planted his feet firmly in the shallow waters of the river, and with one hand, he raised his sword. With the other he raised his shield, now torn and bloody.

As he braced himself for battle, the rumble of hooves and chariot wheels came from behind him. Looking back, he saw an army of Ulstermen, led by Conor Mac Nessa, crest the hill, their banners rippling in the wind, their weapons reflecting the sun.

They tore down the hill to join Cúchulainn at the

ford, where the two armies clashed in a mighty battle which could be heard across all the provinces of Ireland.

Conor Mac Nessa's side seemed to be gaining the upper hand, and soon Maeve's army were on the retreat. She knew her tired troops were no match for Ulster's, but perhaps something could be salvaged from the disaster.

She sent a small band of men away from the battle field on an errand to the Cooley Peninsula.

"With all of Ulster turned out to fight," she said, "the Brown Bull of Cooley will be lightly guarded."

And how right she was. In the chaos of battle, nobody spotted the small group of men cross Ulster's border. They made their way to Cooley, where indeed, they found the bull lightly guarded.

As Maeve's army was retreating, the small group of men dragged the Brown Bull of Cooley out of Ulster by ropes. The thieves took a different route home to avoid Conor Mac Nessa's soldiers, who had successfully driven Maeve's army away.

Back in her Connacht palace, Maeve licked her wounds of defeat, but was cheered by the sight of the gigantic brown bull being hauled kicking, snorting and bellowing into one of her paddocks.

"Don't put him in there!" she shouted at the men.

"Put him with my husband's white bull so that he can see how I've won the argument."

Ailill was brought out to watch the giant brown bull being pushed into an enclosure with his own white bull.

"Happy now?" asked Maeve, smiling.

"Happy, I am not," replied Ailill. "For I cannot believe that my wife would go to war for the sake of winning a stupid argument. I cannot believe my wife would spill the blood of a thousand Connacht men for the sake of this prize."

He pointed at the brown bull, now released from its bonds. Maeve hung her head in shame, but unfortunately the bloodshed wasn't over.

For, in the field, the two bulls eyed each other warily from opposite ends of the paddock. They pawed the ground and snorted disapprovingly. And simultaneously, they lowered their heads, horns pointed forward, and charged across the grass at each other.

They met in an almighty clash, and a violent fight ensued. So closely were the animals matched in strength and size that the fight continued until both bulls fell down dead in the middle of the field.

"Happy now?" Ailill asked his wife in disgust, and turning, he walked away.

The Fenian Cycle

The Fenian Cycle legends, set around the third century, are about the hero Fionn Mac Cumhaill. He was leader of the Fianna, a group of warriors who protected the High King and Ireland's shores from invaders.

Fionn and the Salmon of Knowledge

Near Tara, the seat of the High King of Ireland, flowed the River Boyne. According to legend, a magical fish called the Salmon of Knowledge was said to swim in its waters. Whoever was first to taste the flesh of this fish would have access to the wisdom of the world.

This is the story of the man who ate the Salmon of Knowledge, and used his new power to become one of Ireland's greatest heroes.

Once upon a time, a baby called Deimne was born to a very frightened mother called Muirne. She was hiding because her husband, Cumhall, had been murdered by a one-eyed warrior called Goll. He had killed Cumhall to take his place as leader of the Fianna, an elite group of warriors that guarded the king. Goll vowed to hunt down Cumhall's baby so that he wouldn't grow up to avenge his father's death.

Muirne knew her baby wouldn't be safe with her, so she left him to be raised by handmaidens in the wilds of the Slieve Bloom Mountains.

Deimne was a beautiful baby, with hair as fair as his father's. His handmaidens taught him all the ways of the wild. By the time he was a boy, Deimne could hunt a bird from the sky with a slingshot, and outpace a running deer.

As he got older he sought out company his own age, and one day was lured to the fort of a chieftain by a game of hurling being played by a group of boys. They asked Deimne his name, but the women who cared for him had told him it would be dangerous to reveal his name so he said nothing. So, the boys called him Fionn, which means "fair", because he had hair as golden as sheaves of wheat.

Fionn was given a hurley stick and taught the rules of the game. He picked it up quickly and soon became the best on the pitch. When he returned home, he told the handmaidens how the boys had called him Fionn. They liked the name and started calling him Fionn too. Having a new name might also keep the boy safe from Goll.

Each day, Fionn turned up to play hurling with the boys, and soon word spread about the strength, speed and bravery of this blond-haired boy.

The news reached the ears of Goll, the one-eyed captain of the Fianna who had killed Fionn's father.

"Did you say this boy has fair hair?" Goll asked the messenger.

The messenger nodded. "Yellow, like butter."

Cumhall also had fair hair, thought Goll. *Could this be the child I've been searching for?*

Goll sent his men to capture the boy.

Like Goll, the handmaidens had heard people talking about the blond-haired boy who was brilliant at hurling. They were worried about his safety, so they told him how his father, Cumhall, had once been the leader of the Fianna but had been killed by Goll.

Everyone knew about the Fianna, and Fionn was excited by the possibility of becoming one of them.

"Does that mean I am the rightful leader of the Fianna?" he asked.

The women nodded but told him he needed to become a warrior himself, before he became a captain of warriors. So, Fionn left their care to train with different chieftains in Ireland. He learned how to swing a sword, throw a spear and use a shield to defend himself. Soon he became one of the greatest warriors in the land, gathering his own band of followers, some of whom had been his father's old friends.

Fionn returned to his foster mothers to show off his hard-won battle skills.

"Am I now ready to become leader of the Fianna?" he asked.

"You are indeed a great warrior, Fionn," they said, "but a leader needs to be wise as well as dangerous."

They sent him to the banks of the River Boyne to learn the arts of poetry and storytelling from a wise man called Finnegas.

For seven years, the druid had been fishing in the river in the hope of catching the legendary Salmon of Knowledge. It was said that whoever ate the flesh of this fish would acquire all of the wisdom and knowledge of the world.

Over the seven years he had sought the fish, Finnegas had tried many different methods to catch it, but none had been successful.

Fionn took to his new training quickly. It was certainly easier than the fighting practice he'd undergone with the chieftains. Each morning, Fionn would collect dry wood. Once he had a fire going, he would gather wild fruit, nuts and herbs to be used in the dinner, later that day. Then he would check the fishing lines that Finnegas had set up along the river. He always expected to see the magical salmon dangling from a hook, but mostly he found nothing. If he was lucky he'd find a trout, which he'd gut and clean, and have ready for cooking later on.

Then he would do his study – usually memorizing a poem or story that Finnegas had recited the previous day. Fionn would practise retelling it aloud, while walking up and down the riverbank.

He wouldn't have thought this would be tiring, but after a few hours he always needed a break. Perhaps it was as tiring as training with weapons, but in a different way.

His break would consist of cooking the fish that had been caught earlier. He would build a spit by pressing two Y-shaped branches into the ground on either side of the fire. Then he would skewer the trout on to a third branch and place it on the two Y-shaped branches above the flames. The fish would then be rotated slowly until it was cooked.

Fionn and Finnegas would share the meal of trout, nuts and herbs. Afterwards, Finnegas would recite a new poem or story for Fionn to memorize the following day.

Student and teacher would sleep under the stars, with the sound of the river lulling them to sleep. It was a peaceful, if uneventful life.

One day, Fionn was busy composing a poem when he heard his teacher shouting his name from further down the riverbank. Fionn ran to the old man to see what was the matter. He found Finnegas dancing with joy, holding a huge red-speckled salmon, its scales glittering silver like the moon and its eyes full of wisdom.

"I caught it, my boy!" he shouted. "I finally caught the Salmon of Knowledge."

"That's fantastic news," said Fionn. "What will you do with it?"

Finnegas laughed. "Eat it, of course."

"Shall I cook it for you, master?" asked Fionn. "Or would you prefer to cook this one yourself."

"You've become rather good at the cooking, my boy. So yes, I'd like you to do it." He handed the fish over. "But you must swear that you won't taste the flesh before me."

"I promise," said Fionn.

"Not even the smallest bite," warned Finnegas. "I must be the first to eat it."

Fionn nodded and built a fire, placed the salmon on a spit and then hung it over the flames. The smell of the cooking fish, and the sight of its crisp, golden skin made Fionn's mouth water, but he was a man of his word and kept his promise not to take even a small bite of the salmon.

As Fionn turned the spit, he thought about what it would be like to have all the knowledge of the world. You would always know which direction to take in the woods, which weapon to choose in a fight, and when your enemy was next going to attack. It was a power that could make you very popular with every king in Ireland. It was an ability that could make you a very rich ma—

"Ouch!" shouted Fionn.

He'd been so busy daydreaming that he hadn't been concentrating on the job at hand, and as he was turning the spit, he scorched his thumb on the hot salmon. Immediately, he put his thumb in his mouth to ease the pain. But sucking the throbbing blister on his thumb did more than ease the pain in his thumb – it also gave him the first taste of the fish.

Centuries of knowledge and wisdom flowed through his mind in a torrent of light, image and sound, and Fionn knew that something special had happened to him.

But instead of delight, he felt only guilt. Finnegas had spent years waiting to catch this salmon, and along comes a student and steals that honour away from him. How disappointed Finnegas would be. How betrayed he would feel.

Perhaps if I say nothing, thought Fionn, *and Finnegas eats the salmon, then he'll receive the gift as well as me.*

He decided not to tell Finnegas when he called him for his meal. However, as soon as the teacher saw Fionn, he noticed there was something different about his student. His eyes seemed brighter, deeper and . . . something else. They seemed wiser.

"Did you taste the salmon?" asked Finnegas, a

nervous fear pulling at his face. He looked like he already knew the answer, but was hoping he was wrong.

Fionn swallowed the lump in his throat. He couldn't lie to his teacher. It was bad enough that he'd stolen the man's dreams away, without lying about it too.

He told Finnegas what had happened.

For a long time, Finnegas stared at the ground, speechless. But when he looked up, there was no anger in his eyes, only sadness.

"A prophecy said a fair-haired man would eat the Salmon of Knowledge," he said. "Because my hair was once blond, I thought that would be me, but seemingly not. The gift of knowledge is yours, Fionn, so please, eat the fish."

He handed over the steaming salmon and waited for his student to eat. Fionn, however, had lost his appetite.

"Please eat, my boy," said Finnegas. "Though I am a little sad not to be the chosen one, I am happy that the gift of knowledge has gone to a man of honour such as yourself."

Fionn Mac Cumhaill nodded, ate the fish and received the superpower that had eluded Finnegas for so long. From that day on, whenever Fionn wanted to know what the future held, or he was trying to solve some mystery, he merely had to put his scorched thumb in his mouth and whatever knowledge he required would always come to him. He promised himself that he would only use this power for the good of his fellow people and never for selfish reasons. It was this promise, rather than the power itself, that led Fionn to become one of Ireland's greatest heroes, loved by king and peasant alike.

Fionn and the Fire Demon of Tara

Now that he was a trained warrior, an accomplished poet and had acquired the wisdom of the Salmon of Knowledge, Fionn Mac Cumhaill set out for the High King of Ireland's fort at Tara to become leader of the Fianna, an elite army of the king's. Fionn's father, Cumhall, had once been captain of the Fianna, so Fionn felt the position was his right and destiny.

The road to Tara was busy with bronze and ivory chariots full of warriors, chieftains and kings, for the High King of Ireland had invited them to dine at his table for Samhain, the festival to mark the end of the harvest and the coming of winter.

Fionn arrived at the King's fort and left his weapons outside, as was customary, because Samhain was a time of peace across the land. Fionn joined the throng heading into the king's Great Hall and took a place at one of the tables. Soon, the mead was flowing from silver-rimmed ox horns, platters of crackling roast venison were devoured, and the king's hounds fought over bones on the floor.

At the top table, Fionn saw the High King, and on his right-hand side, a one-eyed warrior. Fionn knew this was Goll, the man who had killed his father to become leader of the Fianna. The sight of his father's murderer made Fionn furious but he kept it under control, knowing that disrupting the feast would mean the end of his invitation.

The Great Hall was alive with the sounds of conversation, laughter and music, but as night drew in, an expectant silence descended on the festivities. Fionn asked the men beside him to explain what was happening, but they shushed him and nodded at the top table, where the king was rising to speak.

"Kings, chieftains and fellow mortals," he said, "I welcome you to Tara. All day we have feasted on fine meat and wine, but as darkness falls the food and drink leave a bitter taste in our mouths, for we know what is coming."

Fionn looked around, dumbfounded. Was he the only one who didn't know what was going on?

Luckily, the king explained. "Samhain, as you all know, is the time of the year when the veil between the worlds of men and spirits becomes so thin that the dead come to haunt us. Every year, a fire demon called Aillen of the Flaming Breath returns from the Otherworld to seek revenge on us men for driving his people, the Tuatha Dé Danann, underground. He wreaks havoc on our fort, burning it to the ground, so that each year we have to build it anew."

A shiver ran down Fionn's spine. Spears, swords and anything else from the world of men, he could handle, but the Otherworld was a different matter. The Tuatha Dé Danann were a treacherous force who fought not only with blades, but with magic. The thoughts of this demon scared him, but surely a single monster could be stopped? Didn't the king have the best weapons, druids and warriors at his disposal?

As if reading Fionn's mind, the king continued. "Though many have tried to stop Aillen, none have succeeded, for this prince of fire plays music on an enchanting harp, lulling to sleep anyone who hears it."

Some of the men looked at each other, nodding as if they'd experienced the enchantment personally.

"If anyone can overcome this demon, he shall have whatever riches he asks for." The king looked around the room expectantly, but nobody volunteered.

The king shook his head and went to sit down, but in an instant, Fionn rose from his seat and said, "I will bring you the head of this creature."

The king squinted his eyes at the fair-haired youth standing before him. "Who are you, boy?"

"I am Fionn, the son of Cumhall."

A collective gasp could be heard in the hall, for many of the men had been friends with Fionn's father and all had heard the rumours that he might have a child. Nobody, however, was more surprised than Goll, whose face went as pale as the moon. Had this boy come to claim leadership of the Fianna and avenge his father's death?

"Stopping Aillen of the Flaming Breath will not be easy," said the king. "But if anybody can do it, it will be a son of Cumhall, for your father was a great man and much loved within these walls."

Fionn looked at Goll, but the man cast his single eye towards the floor.

Spurred on by the king's words, Fionn left the Great Hall, retrieved his weapons and began to pace the high, earthen ditch that surrounded the king's fort.

"I was a friend of your father's," said a voice.

Fionn turned around to find an older man behind him.

"I bring a gift to help you," said the man, holding out a spear, the head of which was covered in a leather sheath.

"I already have a spear," said Fionn.

"Your weapons will be useless against what you will face tonight."

Fionn took the spear. Its haft was made of rowan, darkened by age and polished by many hands. When Fionn took off the leather hood he was surprised to find that the head was not made of iron, but bronze.

"Only a Tuatha Dé Danann spear can kill a Tuatha Dé Danann demon," said the old man.

Fionn raised it above his shoulder and found that it was perfectly balanced, as if it had been made for him.

"It belonged to your father," explained the old man.

"If you've had this spear in your possession for all these years," wondered Fionn, "why have you not used it to kill Aillen yourself?"

"Because I do not know how to use it. Rumour has it that you have knowledge of many things, Fionn Mac Cumhaill."

Fionn knew he was referring to the gift of knowledge that he had obtained by eating the Salmon of Knowledge. He looked at the bronze spear head, the golden rivets of which shone in the moonlight.

Fionn went to thank the old man, but he had already turned his back and was returning to the warmth of the Great Hall.

I wonder... thought Fionn.

He put the thumb that he had scorched on the Salmon of Knowledge in his mouth, and immediately a rush of noise and images filled his mind, and in the middle of it came the wisdom he required – how to use the spear to kill Aillen of the Flaming Breath.

He looked around. Though the gates were closed and the fort was guarded by the king's men, Fionn knew none of this would stop Aillen getting in. The sounds of chatter could be heard faintly in the Great Hall, and beyond it, Tara stretched out like a silver blanket under the moon.

And all the while, Fionn waited and waited. Just when he was beginning to wonder if Aillen would turn up at all, he heard the distant plucking of harp strings ripple through the air, making him feel sleepy. And yet, his heart beat wildly with fear and excitement. If he succeeded in tonight's task, he could demand anything from the king. But if he failed, he would lose everything, including his father's good name and possibly his life. Everything hinged on the magical spear and the knowledge he'd received from sucking his thumb.

It was time to put them to the test. He placed the point of the spear to his forehead, pressing it into his skin until it drew blood. When it did, the sleepiness immediately disappeared and clarity returned to his mind like a cool evening breeze.

The harp music got louder and closer and Fionn

watched the guards crumple into sleep, but he didn't remove the spear from his forehead. As the music reached the king's gate, the last of the noises in the Great Hall disappeared and Fionn knew everyone inside had been put to sleep by the enchanted music.

The fort's gates swung open and there stood Aillen of the Flaming Breath, Prince of the Tuatha Dé Danann, holding a silver harp. He was taller than a human, with flaming red hair which hung in curls around his pointed ears. His mouth was slightly open, and inside it, fire danced and licked his lips. His eyes burned red like two hot coals and his whole body glowed as if lit from within. He seemed surprised to see Fionn awake and watching him.

Fionn decided to use this element of surprise to his advantage and rushed at the beast, the magic spear thrumming to life in his hand. When he reached the demon, Aillen blasted a fiery breath of flame at him, but Fionn rolled under it. He felt the heat of fire on his back but rolled out the other side unharmed, coming to a standing position in front of the monster.

Before Aillen could release another inferno, Fionn thrust the spear deep into the demon's body. The beast squealed in pain and stumbled back to the gate, liquid fire dripping from his wound instead of blood. With a final roar of agony, Aillen turned tail and rushed out the gate, leaving a trail of bloody fire behind him.

Fionn had saved Tara, but that wasn't enough – he'd promised the king this demon's head. He followed the trail of fire and soon caught sight of the injured creature who was heading for a grassy hill. As he got closer, a door in the mound opened, releasing a beam of green light. Fionn knew if the demon escaped through this threshold, the Tuatha Dé Danann would work their healing magic on Aillen and the demon would return to Tara full of vengeance the following Samhain.

Knowing he couldn't catch the demon before he reached safety, Fionn raised the magic spear above his shoulder. He could feel it vibrating with energy like a bird before flight, eager to find its mark. Fionn released the spear, letting it fly, whooshing through the night, swerving around trees and bushes, until it found its target.

With a cry, Aillen of the Flaming Breath crashed to the ground, his light dimming. Immediately, the door to the Otherworld closed and disappeared. The demon had been defeated. All thanks to the magic spear and Fionn's knowledge. Never again would

Samhain be ruined for the king.

With a mighty swing of his sword, Fionn removed the demon's head and brought it back to Tara where everyone had awoken from their stupor, delighted not to find the royal enclosure on fire.

"As promised, Fionn Mac Cumhaill," said the king, "you may name your reward."

"I ask for two things," said Fionn, kneeling. "Firstly, as the son of Cumhall, I ask to take my rightful place as Captain of the Fianna. And secondly, I wish to avenge my father. I challenge Goll to a fight to the death."

The one-eyed warrior stiffened, putting his hand on the hilt of his sword.

The king thought about the request for a long time, before speaking. "I can grant one of your wishes but not the other. You are indeed the rightful leader of the Fianna and you may become its captain, on the condition that you allow Goll Mac Morna to live. Though he has wronged your family, he has been a loyal servant to me and I will not see him needlessly killed. He shall leave Tara and become the head of the Connacht branch of the Fianna so your paths will never cross again. What say you to this, Goll Mac Morna?"

The one-eye warrior bowed his head in acceptance.

"And what say you, Fionn Mac Cumhaill?"

Fionn too, bowed his head and said, "I accept, Your Majesty."

And from that day on, Fionn Mac Cumhaill became not only the leader of the Fianna, but the greatest leader it ever had.

The Giant's Causeway

On the coast of County Antrim there is a geological wonder called the Giant's Causeway. It consists of hexagonal columns of rock which disappear into the sea. According to legend, the rocks were once part of a road or causeway that stretched all the way to Scotland. Indeed, similar rock formations can be found across the water at Fingal's Cave in the Inner Hebrides of Scotland. This is the story of how the Giant's Causeway was built, and then destroyed.

Fionn Mac Cumhaill was the leader of the Fianna, an elite army of warriors who protected the king and the country's shores from invaders. When they weren't fighting, the Fianna loved nothing more than to go hunting.

One day, Fionn was out hunting with the Fianna on the Antrim coast. Some of the men from the group were looking across the sea at Scotland, and talking about the great giant, Benandonner, who lived there.

"They say he can jump over a mountain," said one of the men.

"I bet I could beat him in a fight," boasted Fionn.

"They say he's so tall, his shadow stretches from one end of the Highlands to the other," said one of the other men.

"I could still beat him in a fight," said Fionn, a little less confident this time.

"They say he has the strength of ten men in his little finger," said another of the men.

"I could still beat him," said Fionn, though now he wasn't so sure.

The Fianna liked to goad their captain into accepting challenges because they knew he couldn't back down from one.

"I dare you to shout an insult across the water at the giant," said one of the Fianna.

Fionn was a little scared of upsetting this giant, but he had to maintain a brave face in front of his men, so he accepted the dare.

Climbing to the top of the highest cliff, he shouted, "Come out and show yourself, Benandonner, you big, ugly, cow-dung smelling, fish-faced fool."

The Fianna laughed and whooped, and sure enough, the figure of Benandonner appeared on the distant shore.

"What fool insults me from across the sea?" shouted the Scottish giant.

"I am Fionn Mac Cumhaill, captain of the Fianna," shouted Fionn, now feeling a little braver because his men were encouraging him. It also helped that there was fifty miles of sea between him and the giant. "I challenge you to a fight, you hairy-nosed baboon."

The giant's laugh sounded like thunder rolling across the waves. "If there wasn't a sea between us, I'd come across and squash you with my little finger."

Fionn's men "ooohed" to goad their captain into retaliating. Fionn knew he had to live up to his reputation, so he levered a huge rock out of the ground and flung it at the giant. It landed short, splashing into the sea. People say that the place where Fionn pulled up the rock eventually filled with water and became Lough Neagh, the biggest lake in Ireland. They also say the missile became what we know today as the Isle of Man.

The rock that Fionn had fired gave Benandonner an idea.

"I'm going to build a causeway across the water," he shouted, "and when I cross it I'll hunt you down and crush you under the sole of my boot."

"Fine!" replied Fionn. "I'll build a causeway from my side and meet you halfway."

"Fine!" shouted Benandonner.

Fionn's men had stopped laughing at this stage, now that their game had turned into something dangerously real.

"Are you sure this is a good idea, Fionn?" one of them asked.

"Quit your jabbering," said Fionn, "and give me a hand with these rocks."

So, while Benandonner began tearing great big

chunks of rock from the hillside and flinging them into the sea to form a sort of bridge from Scotland, the Fianna began doing the same on the Irish shore. With their swords, they shaped the rocks from the Irish side into hexagonal columns and planted them in the seabed to form a road across the ocean.

Day by day, the causeway got longer, and soon both sides would meet. As he got closer to Benandonner however, Fionn realized the Scottish giant was indeed as big and as fierce-looking as his men had claimed.

I'll never beat a brute like that in a fight, thought Fionn, *but I can't let my men know this.*

Instead, he came up with another excuse. So, gathering his men around, he said, "We've worked hard, men, and I think we've all earned a break."

The Fianna nodded eagerly in agreement, for like their captain, they were tired and weren't looking forward to meeting the Scottish giant.

"Go home to your families," said Fionn, "and stay there until I send for you."

They nodded happily, and Fionn headed off with them. He hoped that Benandonner would quit working when he saw Fionn's crew wasn't helping.

And even if Benandonner does finish the causeway on his own, thought Fionn. *He'll never find me because he doesn't know where I live.*

Benandonner, however, didn't forget Fionn's insults and was determined to finish the causeway alone.

Fionn Mac Cumhaill returned to his wife, and as soon as she saw his pale complexion she knew something was wrong.

"I've got myself into a bit of bother," he confessed, and told her the whole story.

Stupid men and their bravado, thought Fionn's wife, but she didn't say this aloud.

"I'm worried he'll come after me," said Fionn.

"If this Benandonner comes visiting," said Fionn's wife, "leave him to me. For if I can handle a man like you, Fionn Mac Cumhaill, I can handle any man."

She ordered her husband to go outside and cut wood to make a cradle big enough to fit himself in.

"Why—" began Fionn, but his wife pointed to the door.

Fionn, who might have been brave enough to argue with a giant, never argued with his wife, and so did as he was told.

While he was gone, Fionn's wife stoked the fire

and fetched a sack of flour and nine flat stones. She made ten oatcakes, hiding a flat stone in the centre of nine of them, and marking the tenth with a thumbprint. Then, she baked them over the fire until they were golden.

Meanwhile, Fionn was busy making a cradle big enough to hold a man and, even though he wasn't sure why he was doing it, he trusted whatever plan his wife had in mind.

He had just finished it and had brought it inside when the whole house began to shake. Fionn and his wife looked out the window, and sure enough, the enormous giant, Benandonner, was coming over the hill, flinging trees out of his path. He was every bit as big and fierce as the men of the Fianna had said.

"It's him," squealed Fionn.

"Don't worry," said his wife, handing him an enormous baby's bonnet. "Put this on and climb into the cradle."

Fionn did as he was told, and his wife tucked him under a blanket and told him to suck his thumb. He was barely inside when they heard a knock on the door.

Fionn's wife opened it, but all she could see was a pair of hairy knees. Looking up into the sky, she saw the angry face of Benandonner.

"Is this the home of Fionn Mac Cumhaill?" bellowed the giant.

"It is," said Fionn's wife, "but he's out at the moment. Why don't you come inside and wait for him?"

Benandonner got down on his knees and crawled into the Mac Cumhaill house and sat in the corner. His head touched the ceiling and his legs stretched from one end of the house to the other.

"Would you like some oatcakes?" said Fionn's wife, putting a plate of them before the giant. "They're freshly baked."

Benandonner popped an oatcake in his mouth and then let out a piercing screech.

"Cursing thunder!" he yelled. "What sort of cake is this? It's broken my tooth."

He spat the tooth on to the floor.

"These oatcakes are Fionn's favourites," said his wife. "He likes them crispy. Here, have a softer one."

She handed him another cake and the same thing happened. This time, the giant spat out two teeth.

"They're as hard as stone!" shouted Benandonner.

"Fionn eats them every day," said his wife. "Even the baby eats them."

This was Fionn's cue to make a "goo, goo, gaa, gaa" noise from the cradle.

Fionn's wife handed the oatcake marked with a thumbprint to the "baby" in the cradle, and Fionn gobbled it down in seconds.

If the baby can eat these cakes, what sort of man must his father be? thought Benandonner, now starting to regret ever coming to the house.

"What age is the baby?" asked the giant, thinking that the cradle was very big.

"Just eight months," said Fionn's wife.

Benandonner peered into the cradle at Fionn. "He's very big."

"He takes after his father," said Fionn's wife.

If the baby is this big, thought Benandonner, *his father must be huge.*

"Can the baby talk yet?" asked the giant.

"No, but he can cry so loud he disturbs the birds of Munster. Fionn can't bear to hear him crying. He'd kill anyone who upset his baby."

Again, Fionn took this as his cue to roar as loud as he could.

"Quick!" said Fionn's wife to Benandonner. "Let the baby suck your little finger. Fionn will be in such a temper if he comes home and hears the baby crying."

The giant put his little finger in Fionn's mouth.

Fionn remembered his Fianna warriors saying that the giant had the strength of ten men in his little finger.

Let's see if this is true, thought Fionn, biting down on the finger as hard as he could.

His teeth crunched through the bone, cutting the finger clean off.

The giant bellowed in pain, and bolted from the house as fast as he could.

If Fionn Mac Cumhaill's baby can injure me this much, he thought as he bounded across hilltops and forests, *I'd hate to see what the baby's father could do. He must be twice as big as me, twice as tough and twice as mean.*

When he reached the causeway, he tore across it, ripping up the rocks as he went so that Fionn couldn't follow.

Meanwhile, Fionn climbed out of the cradle, took off the baby bonnet, and kissed his wife.

"I'm so lucky to have such a clever wife," he told her. "If it wasn't for you, I'd have been squashed like a fly under the boot of Benandonner."

"Don't you forget it, Fionn Mac Cumhaill," she

said, smiling. "A great Irish hero is only as good as the wife that saves his bacon."

The Birth of Oisín

Fionn Mac Cumhaill had two favourite hunting dogs called Bran and Sceolán. He trusted them as if they were family, and in a way, they were. You see, the dogs' mother had once been human – Fionn's aunt, in fact. While pregnant, she had been turned into a dog by a witch, and later gave birth to her twins in the shape of dogs. Fionn named them Bran and Sceolán and their strange heritage made them much more than ordinary dogs.

One day, Fionn Mac Cumhaill was out hunting with the Fianna and his two dogs, Bran and Sceolán. They'd roamed the plains of Kildare all day but had no luck catching anything, and were heading back to Fionn's fort on the Hill of Almu. They were almost there when a dappled deer sprung out from the ferns, right into their path.

The hind's dark eyes looked out at Fionn from under long lashes, and then it skipped away again. It was almost asking to be chased, and there were no better dogs to do it than Bran and Sceolán. They took off after the deer, bounding over rotting logs and crashing through undergrowth.

Fionn followed, sounding his hunting horn so that the rest of the Fianna and dogs could follow. His horse struggled to keep up with Bran and Sceolán, who were heading straight towards the Hill of Almu. Fionn thought this was strange – wild animals usually kept a wide berth of human dwellings and he'd expected the deer to head deeper into the forest.

The deer, the dogs and Fionn were moving so fast through the forest that they soon left the rest of the hunting party far behind. Bursting through the alder trees at the edge of the forest, Fionn and his horse emerged onto the open grassland surrounding the Hill of Almu. Fionn was flabbergasted at what he saw.

The hind lay in the grass, panting with exertion from its sprint, and on either side of it lay Bran and Sceolán, licking its face and trembling limbs as if the deer was a brother or sister.

Fionn pulled his horse up short of this extraordinary scene, knowing that there must be something special about this deer if his hounds cared for it so tenderly.

When the rest of the Fianna and their dogs arrived on the scene, Bran and Sceolán stood protectively in front of the deer, teeth bared and snarling. Fionn wheeled round his horse and ordered his men to call their dogs off.

"It was as if this deer was trying to find refuge," explained Fionn, nodding towards his white-walled fortress on the hill. "And no guest of mine, even a deer, will come to harm on my property."

And with that, the day's hunting was called off. Fionn led the party up the hill for some much-needed rest. The deer followed, Bran and Sceolán never leaving her side. She even lay with the dogs at Fionn's feet while he ate supper.

Fionn woke in the middle of the night at the sound of an opening door. Light flooded in from the torches outside, and standing in the centre of it was the most beautiful woman he had ever seen. She had pale skin and hair so blonde it was almost white. Her eyes were unusually dark with long lashes. When he saw her ears, which were slightly pointed, Fionn knew she was not human. She was of the Sídhe, the Fairy Kind, the Tuatha Dé Danann.

"I must be dreaming," he said, rubbing his eyes.

"This is no dream, Fionn Mac Cumhaill," said the woman. "My name is Sadhbh and I am the deer that you chased in the forest yesterday."

Speechless, Fionn sat up in his bed.

"The Dark Druid of my own tribe wanted to marry me," continued Sadhbh, "and when I refused, he put an enchantment upon me, turning me into a deer. One of the druid's servants took pity on me and told me the spell could be broken if I slept in the fort of Fionn Mac Cumhaill."

"Bran and Sceolán must have known this," said Fionn.

"They sensed it because they too are creatures of

enchantment."

"My home is your home," said Fionn. "For as long as you decide to stay, you will have my protection."

Sadhbh did stay, and made herself useful, helping out in whatever way she could. As the days went by, Fionn fell more and more in love with Sadhbh. Though well aware of the dangers of getting involved with the Sídhe, Fionn proposed to Sadhbh, and they were married. Fionn was so much in love that for a while, he neglected his duties as captain of the Fianna, and even stopped hunting. His men were worried that he was getting soft.

One day, however, a call came to his door that he could not ignore.

"War-ships are approaching from the northern sea," said the king's messenger.

"Please don't go," begged Sadhbh to her husband.

"I must," said Fionn. "I am captain of the Fianna, and our duty is to protect Ireland's shores. I will leave men to guard you, my love. You will be safe as long as you stay within these walls."

With that, Fionn rounded up the Fianna from the five provinces of Ireland, and rode out with freshly sharpened weapons for Dublin Bay.

There, they fought the invaders for seven days,

finally driving them back into the sea. Those that didn't escape had their ships burned as a warning to their fleeing comrades not to return.

Battle-weary, Fionn rode back to the Hill of Almu, expecting to see his beautiful wife looking out for him over the walls, but there was no sign of her, and an uneasiness coiled in his stomach. When he saw the downcast faces of his guards he knew something had happened. One of them explained.

"Three days after you left, we saw a figure that looked exactly like you, returning up the hill with Bran and Sceolán. The Lady Sadhbh was so excited to tell you some sort of news that she pushed open the gates and rushed out to meet you. The person we thought was you threw off his disguise to reveal the robes of a druid underneath. With a hazel wand, the druid turned your wife into a deer, and led her, enchanted, into the forest. We grabbed our weapons and rushed after them, but no trace of the deer, the dogs or the druid could be found."

By now, the colour had drained from Fionn's face. He didn't speak, but shut himself away in his room, refusing company, food and drink. On the third day, he emerged to take up his duties as captain of the Fianna, but in every spare moment, he searched for Sadhbh.

For seven years he scoured the four corners of Ireland with Bran and Sceolán, but to no avail. He'd all but given up on ever finding his wife again, when one day he was hunting with the Fianna, and he heard the dogs making a terrible racket ahead. He parted the foliage to find them surrounding a naked boy, who looked to be around seven years old.

Bran and Sceolán stood protectively before the boy, snarling at the other dogs. Fionn had witnessed this exact scene before, so he called off the dogs and knelt before the boy.

"What's your name, boy?" Fionn asked the child.

The boy, whose hair was as fair as Fionn's but had eyes as dark as bog pools, didn't seem to understand the question, or the others which followed. When he tried to speak, all that came out were grunting noises. Fionn held out his hand and eventually the boy took it, and together they returned to Almu.

It wasn't easy for the boy to adapt to a new way of living. Fionn gave him a bed but the boy preferred the floor. When Fionn gave him clothes, the boy ripped them off. When a meal was placed before him, he took it under the table and ate it with the dogs.

Bit by bit, however, the boy began to adopt the habits of Fionn and his men. He listened to the

Fianna's conversations, picking up new words every day and trying them out in his mouth, as if tasting exotic foods.

After a year, he was almost like any of the other boys in Almu, except his eyes held a dark sadness that Fionn never asked about. He waited for the boy to offer it up willingly. And one day, he did.

Sitting between Bran and Sceolán in front of a roaring fire, the boy told Fionn his story.

His earliest memories were of being cared for by a deer. She gave him milk when he was thirsty and kept him warm on winter nights. They lived on fruit and berries, and the boy wasn't aware that the deer was different to him in any way.

One day, they were visited by a man in dark robes and carrying a hazel stick. Usually they steered clear of humans, but the boy's mother seemed to know this man, though she was wary of him because she stood protectively in front of her son. The man spoke to her in strange words, but the boy's mother just shook her head, which sent the man away in anger.

Many times, the robed stranger returned, often seeming to plead and beg the hind, but she always turned away, back to her son.

One day, the man became so angry that he waved

his hazel rod at the deer, putting her into a trance and leading her away into the trees. When the boy tried to follow, his mother shook her head, telling him to stay put.

For days, he waited for her to return. When she didn't, he went searching for her, but it was as if she'd disappeared into another world. The boy learned to live alone, hunting for himself until the day the Fianna found him.

Fionn listened to the story with joy, knowing that the boy's mother was his wife, Sadhbh. Tears of both sadness and joy flowed down his cheeks as the boy spoke because although Fionn had lost a wife, he'd gained a son he never knew existed.

He called the boy Oisín, which means *little fawn*, and he grew up to be one of the Fianna's greatest champions. Renowned for his poetry, singing and storytelling, he became a leader of men. They respected him, but kept him at arm's length too, because there was an otherworldliness about Oisín that frightened them. Perhaps it was his slightly pointed ears or dark, sad eyes, but most probably it was because he had the blood of the Fairy Kind flowing through his veins.

Oisín in Tír na n-Óg

Many countries have a legend about a hero going to another world, only to return hundreds of years later. In Japan, it's the tale of Urashima Tarō; in Britain, it's the story of King Herla; and in Ireland, it's the legend of Oisín in Tír na n-Óg (The Land of Youth).

Fionn Mac Cumhaill and the Fianna were out hunting among the lakes of Killarney. The sun sparkled off the water and warmed the men's bones. They stopped to watch a rider approach from a distant hill, and as it got closer were surprised to see that it was a beautiful woman with long golden hair tied into plaits.

Her blue eyes reflected the sunlight, making them sparkle. She wore a cloak embroidered with yellow stars, and rode a magnificent white horse, saddled and shod in silver.

"I'm looking for Fionn Mac Cumhaill, Captain of the Fianna," said the woman.

"Well, look no further," said Fionn, "for I am the man you seek. And who, pray tell, might you be?"

"I am Niamh of the Golden Hair, daughter of the King of Tír na n-Óg."

"How may I be of service, Princess Niamh of the Golden Hair?" asked Fionn, brushing his hair back off his forehead.

"Actually, it's your son, Oisín, I'm looking for."

"Oh." Fionn looked a bit disappointed. "How do

you know my son?"

"I don't," said Niamh. "But I have heard of his bravery, kindness and skills in the arts of music, poetry and storytelling."

Oisín, who had been listening to the conversation with the rest of the Fianna, couldn't believe what he was hearing. The most beautiful woman he'd ever seen was asking about him.

Fionn, always protective of his son, asked, "And what might your business be with Oisín?"

"My father, the king, wants me to find a husband."

"And are there no eligible men in Tír na n-Óg?"

"There are plenty," said Niamh, "but since I heard the stories of Oisín, I couldn't stop thinking about him. I had to come and see him for myself."

Oisín couldn't hold his tongue any longer.

He brought his horse out into the clearing and said, "I am Oisín."

Niamh blinked her eyes. "You are indeed as handsome as the stories say. What say you? Would you like to become my husband? If you come with me, you will one day rule Tír na n-Óg, a land where nobody grows old and nobody dies. You will have food a plenty, a towering castle, a hundred swords, a hundred cattle, a hundred sheep, a hundred hunting dogs, a hundred loyal servants and a hundred brave warriors."

Oisín knew he couldn't refuse such an offer. He was so blinded by Niamh's beauty that he didn't stop to consider the price of acceptance – that he would have to leave his family, friends and home behind.

"There is only one thing I want," he replied, "and she's sitting on a horse before me."

He moved towards her, but Fionn put out his hand to stop him. "Oisín, my precious son, please do not go. If you do, I fear I will never see you again."

"Father, I can tell already, this is the woman I was meant to marry. If I do not go, my heart will crack down the middle," Oisin said, his eyes bright with love.

Fionn nodded, for he understood true love – he'd felt the same way about Oisín's mother. Fionn was also aware that his son was part Sídhe, and a mortal wife could never satisfy him the way this eternal princess could.

"Promise me you'll return," he begged his son. "I couldn't bear the thought of never seeing you again."

"I promise," said Oisín, but his mind was on his beautiful bride-to-be, and he took Niamh's hand and climbed on to the saddle behind her without a backwards glance at his father.

The pair galloped across hills and woodland until they reached the shores of the ocean. Their horse never broke its stride when it reached the sea, but continued its light-footed gallop over the waves, its hooves barely touching the water. With Niamh's perfumed hair blowing in his face, Oisín watched Ireland shrink into the distance until they were surrounded by sea.

After a while, land appeared on the horizon, growing larger with every splash of the horse's hooves. A rich green island appeared before them with sandy beaches overlooked by an ivory castle. Crowds lined the strand, cheering and waving flags at the approaching riders.

The horse slowed and came to a halt on the sand, and Oisín, saddle-sore and weary, dismounted and helped Niamh down from the horse. The people seemed overjoyed to see their princess.

They fell silent when a man, who could only have been Niamh's father, parted the crowd. He wore a red cloak and a sparkling crown of gold.

He hugged his daughter and bowed to Oisín. "Welcome to Tír na n-Óg, my prince."

Oisín returned the bow. He'd never been called a

prince before.

Only a few days later, Niamh and Oisín were married. The banquet, lasting seven days and seven nights, had the finest of food, wine and music. The guests danced so much they fell asleep right there on the dance floor, and when they woke, the party continued.

The people of Tír na n-Óg were all young and healthy. Nobody got old, nobody got sick, nobody died. There was no war, murder or crime of any sort. It was truly a paradise in every way.

As the years went by, Niamh and Oisín continued to be as happy as the day they were married, but Oisín began to grow homesick. He missed his father and the Fianna and their hunting expeditions. He asked Niamh if he could return home for a visit.

Her heart ached to see her husband upset, but she knew if he returned to Ireland he might never return. She loved him too much to lose him, so instead she distracted him with kisses, gifts and plans for their future. She encouraged him to put all memories of Ireland out of his head. The more he tried, however, the stronger the memories grew, until his whole demeanour became wracked by loneliness. He became a shadow of the man that

Niamh had married, and she knew she had to do something about it.

"Even if you did go back," she said, "it wouldn't be the same. Ireland will have changed."

"I don't care," said Oisín, brightening at the idea of returning. "I just want to see the place again."

"You may take my horse and go," she said, "under one condition."

Oisín nodded.

"You must promise not to leave your saddle once you get there."

"I promise."

"I mean it, Oisín. You mustn't touch your feet on Ireland's soil."

She knew this was important because her own father had asked her to make the same promise when she'd gone to Ireland the first time. She knew something bad would happen if Oisín got off his horse.

He laughed and told her not to worry. Then he kissed her and ran to the stables to saddle up Niamh's white horse.

As she watched Oisín gallop away across the waves, Niamh felt an emotion she'd never experienced before – anxiety. Deep in her heart, she knew her husband was on a dangerous quest, but there was nothing she could do about it.

The horse's hooves caressed the water so gently they barely made a splash, and soon the emerald shores of Ireland appeared ahead. Oisín couldn't wait to see his father and all his friends in the Fianna, so he galloped up the beach and across the hills in search of them.

He couldn't believe how much the place had changed since he'd left. Many of the forests had been cleared and turned into farmland with enclosures full of sheep and cattle. Strange stone crosses and buildings with narrow windows, spires and bell towers dotted the landscape. Oisín had no idea what they could be for.

He was equally shocked when he met some people. They were small and weak-looking, and nothing like the Celtic people he remembered living with. When he asked them about Fionn and the Fianna, they cowered and shook their heads. To them, Oisín looked like a god, all muscle and golden locks.

Frustrated, he decided to head to the Hill of Almu where Fionn lived, but instead of a white-walled citadel, he found a crumbling ruin, overgrown with ragwort and nettles.

Where is everyone? wondered Oisín. *And what has*

happened to this place?

He decided to ride to Tara, because if anybody knew where Fionn might be, it would be the High King of Ireland.

On his way, he passed through the Valley of the Thrushes, not far from where Dublin stands today. He came upon a group of men trying to move a boulder from a field they were ploughing. There must have been ten men in total, but they hadn't managed to shift the rock even the tiniest bit.

Their mouths dropped open when they saw Oisín approach. One of the men made a series of strange movements with his right hand, touching his forehead, his chest, and then each of his shoulders.

"Do you want some help?" asked Oisín, pointing at the boulder.

The men nodded fearfully, but Oisín, remembering Niamh's warning, didn't leave his saddle. The rock was so small anyway, that he knew he'd be able to lift it without getting off his horse.

He leaned down, and with one hand, scooped the rock out of the earth and flung it into a nearby ditch. The villagers were so transfixed by this feat of strength that their eyes followed the arc of the rock through the air. They didn't see the girth of

Oisín's saddle snap. They didn't see the son of Fionn Mac Cumhaill fall to the ground, touching the soil of Ireland, just as Niamh had warned him not to.

Upon touching the ground, Oisín's body curled up into a ball. His bones began to shrink, leaving his skin loose and wrinkly. Teeth, hair and muscle all disappeared in an instant.

By the time the villagers had returned their focus to Oisín, he'd turned into a frail old man.

"I knew he was a fairy," whispered one of the onlookers, drawing back in terror.

One of the braver men knelt down beside Oisín and said, "Who are you?"

"I am Oisín, son of Fionn Mac Cumhaill."

"You can't be. Fionn Mac Cumhaill and the Fianna all died three hundred years ago."

Oisín was speechless. It had only felt like he'd been in Tír na n-Óg for a short time. How had three hundred years passed in Ireland?

Niamh did warn him that the place would have changed. Perhaps she knew, and that's why she didn't want him to go.

"The old man is dying," said one of the villagers. "Let's take him to the priest."

Together, they carried the frail Oisín to the priest,

Patrick, who told him the story of the new religion that had come to Ireland. Oisín learned that the stone buildings he'd seen were the churches where the people of Christianity prayed.

Before he died, Oisín in turn, told Patrick stories of Fionn Mac Cumhaill and the Fianna, and his beloved Niamh of the Golden Hair in Tír na n-Óg. Patrick wrote them all down with a quill and ink, and this is why we have these stories today.